A Morning in the Life of Henry Faulkner

A Two-Act Play

By

John Preston

Pub This Press
One South Florence Terrace
Sarasota, FL 34237

www.pubthis.com

Printed in the United States of America

To the Memory of Henry

Custom is that little town near hell.
—BBB

A Morning in the Life of Henry Faulkner
A Two-Act Play
By
John Preston

CHARACTERS:
HENRY FAULKNER—AN ARTIST
HOLLIS McCREARY—A HOUSEGUEST
STELLA BAYNES—A LOCAL FRIEND
ANDREW MAYHAN—A BRIEF VISITOR
EVA LIMING—HOLLIS' GIRLFRIEND
JACK FARLEY—A SAILOR

PLACE:
The front room of FAULKNER'S house in Key West, Florida—a few quality antiques, an arrangement of shabby vintage furniture, an accumulation of roadside salvage (e.g., a paint-chipped Doric porch post in the corner under the stairs).

TIME:
The mid-1960s, a sunny morning in late January.

RISE:

Enter forty-year-old, impish HENRY FAULKNER through kitchen doorway, smiling and humming a bluesy melody as he carries a cardboard box to a large table beside an open window (through which the sun-lit foliage of a night-blooming jasmine seems to be leisurely reaching into the room). This is a bright, yellowy nook where most of the lighting is concentrated—the morning sun. After setting the box down on the table he abruptly turns and strides back out. Being small and energetic, his movements and gestures are quick and to the point, to the extent of causing his reddish blond head of soft, feathery curls to bounce and sway as he moves. What one is sure to notice as he exits is that his slightly soiled white trousers are a little too short, and that his long-sleeved, faded madras shirt is a little too large.

 After a moment, HOLLIS McCREARY comes out of his bedroom near the foot of the stairs carrying a small gray kitten, which he cuddles in the crook of his arm as he tiptoes halfway up the stairs and cocks his head to listen. HOLLIS is a nineteen-year-old college dropout who has chanced upon HENRY in a wild pursuit for something more than the ordinary. He wears only a pair of cut-off jeans, hanging low on his slender hips.

At this instant HENRY re-enters carrying another box, still humming but beginning to sing the words now in a slight southern mountain drawl. After placing this second box on the table, he suddenly pivots to catch HOLLIS making a quiet retreat from the stairs.

HENRY:

Just what—are you doing, Hollis?

HOLLIS:

[caught!] Nothing. Just checking…

HENRY:
[a light snort] Hmm…checking for what?

HOLLIS:
[shrugs] Just seeing if I could hear anything, I guess.

HENRY:
The word for that is eavesdropping, you know.

HOLLIS:
Yeah, I know. *Technically*. But—

HENRY:
I don't think listening in on them was part of the deal.

HOLLIS:
[apologetically] Well—I didn't hear anything. If that counts?

HENRY:
Not even the bed springs squeaking? [sly grin]

HOLLIS:
[a worried look toward the top of the stairs] I didn't hear a sound, Henry.

HENRY:
Well, maybe they're resting.

HOLLIS:
Resting? Why would they be resting?

HENRY:
I don't know, Hollis. Why does anybody rest? They get tired. [to this, HOLLIS looks perplexed and silently mouths the word *tired*.] And what are you doing with that kitten in here?

You know perfectly well I don't want any of them back inside the house until it's absolutely safe. You haven't let him down on the floor have you?

HOLLIS:
No, I've been holding him. It's the little one-eyed one. He was crying under my window and I reached out and picked him up. He must have gotten off the porch somehow.

HENRY:
I thought you fixed all the holes in the screen?

HOLLIS:
I did. I fixed all the holes I could find.

HENRY:
Well, obviously not all of them. I don't want anything else getting out, Hollis.

HOLLIS:
[obediently] Well, I'll go look again. [to the kitten as he starts out] Let's go, Cyclops.

HENRY
I wish you would please stop calling him that!

HOLLIS:
[halts] It sort of suits him—Cyclops.

HENRY
No it doesn't. You're merely making fun of him. Let me see him. [takes kitten and examines its eye] Hmm…I'm certain he was born this way. It's completely clouded over. Let me see…what is the name of the blind man in the bible?

HOLLIS:

I don't think the blind man had a name.

HENRY:

Yes, he has a name. I'm quite positive.

HOLLIS:

There were several blind men—but they were all anonymous, just people in the crowd who followed him around.

HENRY:

I'm thinking about the persistent one—whom the crowd kept pushing aside. Surely you remember the story? He was the only *real* Christian in the bunch if you ask me.

HOLLIS:

Oh—yeah—the one that kept *buggin'* Jesus, you mean?

HENRY:

Yes. But what was his name? [gives kitten back to HOLLIS] Here. Take him back out to the others. Maybe the name will come to me later on.

HOLLIS:

Okay. [as he exits kitchen door] But he's only blind in one eye.

HENRY:

[statement of fact] That's practically blind for a cat, don't you know—
[HENRY turns back to the boxes and removes a load papers and books from one of them and begins sorting it all out on the table. He stops to leaf through an old art book he finds interesting, seems to be engrossed in it for a moment. HOLLIS re-enters without the kitten.]

HOLLIS:

Henry…

HENRY:

[still leafing through book] What now, Hollis? Did you find the hole already?

HOLLIS:

It wasn't a hole after all. As soon as I set him down he headed for the crack in the screen door that was a little open. I pulled it all the way shut. He was the only one small enough to squeeze through it somehow. I think it needs a new spring.

HENRY:

Well, I can't be bothered with that right now. Try tying a knot in it. We did that all the time back home. It'll work that way for a while.

HOLLIS:

I already did. We used to have to do that too.

HENRY:

[after a short pause in which HOLLIS looks up at the stair landing and frowns] Well—is there something else…?

HOLLIS:

Well—I was just thinking. I could go ahead and look the name of the blind man up in the Bible if you want me to?

HENRY:

I would have suggested that myself a moment ago, but my only Bible is upstairs in my room. Unless you have one?

HOLLIS

All I have like that is a dictionary. [looks toward upstairs landing again] But if they're just *resting*, maybe I could run up and have one of them hand it out to me.

HENRY:

[turning to look at him] I don't think Jack would appreciate that. Nor Eva either, for that matter. Furthermore, it's just a pretext isn't it, an excuse to go up there?

HOLLIS:

[shrugs] Maybe they're through. They've had enough time. I didn't hear anything.

HENRY:

I think they'll let us know when they're through. What does a little while longer matter?

HOLLIS:

I just think they've had plenty enough time to do it, is all.

HENRY:

Well, maybe they're doing it again.

HOLLIS:

Again? But—I don't think Eva would go for that…

HENRY:

I think Jack wanted her very badly. You can't blame him for taking advantage of the situation, can you?

HOLLIS:

Yeah, but I don't think Eva was expecting that.

HENRY:

Well, it's a little too late to do anything about it now. Why don't you take a walk or something. I think you need to distract yourself now.

HOLLIS:

No, I think I'll just wait and walk her back home when they're through.

HENRY:

Suit yourself. But I don't understand why you are starting to act this way. You're creating too much tension over this now and it's not good.

HOLLIS:

[looking toward the landing] Yeah. Maybe you're right, Henry. Why should I worry about some little whore?

HENRY:

Well, Hollis! I don't think calling her names is—is going to help you much.

HOLLIS:

I know. I guess I didn't mean to say that.

HENRY:

I'm sure you didn't. But you're over-reacting to this now; you need to just put it out of your mind and go about your business. Go in your room and work if nothing else. Who knows, maybe this will give you something new to write about. Think of it that way.

HOLLIS:

I already did. Maybe that's why I did it in the first place.

HENRY:

Well, there you go. Writers are well known for creating their own conflict. [sly grin]

HOLLIS:

If that's what it takes, I'm an expert at that, I guess.

HENRY:

Yes. I agree.

HOLLIS:

I will be a great writer someday, Henry.

HENRY:

[busy at table, removes more material from boxes] That remains to be seen. But who knows, it's all up to you.

HOLLIS:

The key is to never give up, no matter what it takes. I've made that vow.

HENRY:

One needs to read and study all the old masters, too, you know.

HOLLIS:

I've read quite a few of them already. Mostly on my own, besides college.

HENRY:

Well, I hope you don't regret leaving college someday.

HOLLIS:

I'm not worried about that. After they told me I was the first freshman in the history of the college to win the Dixie Lee Green Writing Contest, I thought there was no place else to go but down. I bet I'm the only person who's ever been proud of getting accused of plagiarism in college. But the professor apologized and changed my grade to an A after I won. Then she said she expected to read me someday—in front of the whole class.

HENRY:

Well, the people who help you early on are the ones you'll always remember, I think. But—

HOLLIS:

[cutting in] Yeah, she begged me not to quit. She said the award just showed I had future talent. But talent is talent, I say.

HENRY:

Well, I just love her name. Dixie Lee Green.

HOLLIS:

No, she was Doctor Lindsey. My writing teacher.

HENRY:

Then who was Dixie Lee Green? I think the name compels one to ask.

HOLLIS:

[shrugs] Probably some old dead English teacher before my time that they named the contest for.

HENRY:

You don't know?

HOLLIS:

No. Not really.

HENRY:

Well, she sounds interesting.

HOLLIS:

Nobody mentioned who she was. I just figured she was

somebody important some way to the college.

HENRY:

Yes, I suppose.

HOLLIS:

I was so excited about winning and all—

HENRY:

Well, you are quite, quite self-absorbed, Hollis. I understand.

HOLLIS:

Self-absorbed?

HENRY:

Yes.

HOLLIS:

But I always think of other people first. That's why I always get the short end of the stick. All I know is I can't say *no* to anybody.

HENRY:

Well, all that does is simply make you a fool on top of being self-absorbed.

HOLLIS:

Well—[Shrugs]—in relation to being self-absorbed—what about Eva—upstairs? What is that?

HENRY:

That's just a minor way of paying me back for room and board. And I do feed good, as you well know.

HOLLIS:

Yeah, I know, Henry. I appreciate it. If it wasn't for you I'd probably be out on the streets. But I'm just saying that in relation to being self-absorbed she is my girlfriend after all.

HENRY:

What's that supposed to mean? Other than what it means.

HOLLIS:

Well…it's just that…I'm providing her, you know…and…

HENRY:

[with airs]Yes, but you're only providing the *hole*, Jack's providing the *pole*!

HOLLIS:

Well—the pole ain't no good without the hole, is it?

HENRY:

I'm afraid you have that backwards, Hollis. Most people do. But is that what you're really worried about? Jack's pole? [sly grin]

HOLLIS:

If it's big as you say it is, I guess I am. All I'm saying is that they've been up there way over thirty minutes. What's taking so long?

HENRY:

Nobody said anything about a time limit.

HOLLIS:

I know, but I didn't think it was going to take but a little while. That's all Eva was expecting.

HENRY:

If you think that, Hollis, you know very little about what women expect.

HOLLIS:

All I know is that she didn't really want to do this. I made her. So it's not like she's supposed to enjoy it. I thought Jack kind of understood that.

HENRY:

The poor man misses his wife—at least that's how he put it to me. And he is shipping out on a long cruise tomorrow, so I wouldn't begrudge him for taking his time.

HOLLIS:

I'm not begrudging him, Henry. I just think it's weird! I can't believe he's up there *pretending* she's his wife! Whoever heard of that? Man!

HENRY:

Is that any worse than you? Down here pretending you care more than you really do?

HOLLIS:

But I do really care. It hurt her feelings when I made her do this. You didn't see the look on her face as she went up the stairs—and the look she gave me before she went in.

HENRY:

Well, are you feeling guilty now—or jealous—or what?

HOLLIS:

I kind of feel sorry for her now, I guess.

HENRY:

When I first took you in you bragged that you had a girlfriend, but that you were just using her. Is that not still the case?

HOLLIS:

Well, just because I said that doesn't mean I don't like her. I do like her. [shrugs]

HENRY:
Then you like her because she's useful?

HOLLIS:
Yeah. Sexually useful, yeah. She's not very well educated, you know.

HENRY:
No, I wouldn't know—you've hardly ever brought her around.

HOLLIS:
I just thought she might bug you or something.

HENRY:
She doesn't steal, does she?

HOLLIS:
No. She's not like that.

HENRY:
You're sure?

HOLLIS:
Yeah, I'm sure. She's just kind of shy. That makes her look shifty. She's pretty though.

HENRY:
She's kind of cute in the face, but she's plump. A little piggish.

HOLLIS:
[hurt] She may be just a little bit overweight, but she still has a good shape.

HENRY:

Well, anyway, she's certainly come in handy this morning, bless her heart.

HOLLIS:

I said I could do it.

HENRY

Yes, you did.

HOLLIS:

[begrudgingly] I hope Jack's happy now.

HENRY:

I had to do something for him. He seemed quite desperate… on the verge of breaking down or something. He wouldn't even get out of bed this morning.

HOLLIS:

Yeah, but I don't understand why he *couldn't wait*—why he had to have her right now? She's never even given *me* any this early in the morning.

HENRY:

All I know is what I've already told you. He simply woke up this morning and asked me if I knew any women. He seemed very distressed about it.

HOLLIS:

Why is he so nervous all the time? Like a cat on a hot tin roof or something—only he's a guy.

HENRY:

It's the navy. There's something about the navy that he can't deal with, I think.

HOLLIS:

Well, if that's the case, why did he re-enlist?

HENRY:

He says it's for the bonus money. That's how they entice you to stay in, you know.

HOLLIS:

It wouldn't entice me—not with Vietnam going on.

HENRY:

Well, he's shipping out to the Mediterranean. So he'll be far away from that, thank God.

HOLLIS:

My father tried to get me to join the Air Force. That's when I tried to get him to help me out with college. He said I should go in the service instead, and learn a trade so that I would be able to get a job when I got out. Man—that about killed me. For him to think I would settle to just learn a trade in life, like being a sheet-metal worker or something. That was some fucking advice!

HENRY:

Well, I have some advice for you too, Hollis. I'm going to be busy here and I don't want to be disturbed for a while. Why don't you go out back and do something. See about Alice. I don't want her to get low on water; it's starting to get warm now.

HOLLIS:

Okay. I'll put her in the shed out of the sun for a while.

HENRY:

That'll be fine. But don't force her if she doesn't want to—

HOLLIS:

[looking toward stairs] Well, I'll give them a little while longer. But I don't understand what's taking so long.

HENRY:

They're fucking, Hollis.

[HOLLIS exits kitchen doorway with a grimace. HENRY remains at the table, facing audience. He will busy himself throughout the rest of the play sorting out the two boxes, selecting images and motifs from long-forgotten sketches that promise possibilities, occasionally picking up a pencil to make a note or to add a line to a drawing. He will rarely stray from this task unless he becomes engaged in other direct action demanding all his attention. Although he is the central character in the play, this preoccupation will make it appear as if he is merely making comments from the sidelines. As he picks up another bundle of papers, the foliage in the open window catches his eye and he leans over to take several deep breaths of outside air. During this, a light knock is heard at the open front door, and a husky female voice calls in: "Well, if the mountain won't come to Mohammed...." STELLA BAYNES enters. She is a richly tanned, self-assured woman in her late fifties, wearing a bright-flowered sundress and carrying a large canvas shoulder bag.]

HENRY:

[accommodating smile] Well—Stella.

STELLA:

[cheerfully] How're you doing, Henry?

HENRY:

I'm doing alright. How are you?

STELLA:

I can't complain. It's another glorious day in the southernmost city!

HENRY:

Yes it is, isn't it? God is smiling from ear to ear today.

STELLA:

Ha—I would say so. What's going on with you, dear? You look busy.

HENRY:

I'm looking through some old stuff, trying to come up with some ideas. I've got a show coming up in less than a month and I need several more paintings.

STELLA:

Oh, well, I won't stay but a minute, if you don't mind? [Without waiting for an answer, she weaves her way over to a stuffed armchair near him, sits and digs in her bag for cigarettes.] Another Palm Beach show, I presume?

HENRY:

No. I'm showing in Naples next. I've never shown there before. I'm a little excited about it. I've heard the gallery is going to advertise in the *New York Times*.

STELLA:

[sighs and pulls out the pack] It must be nice, dear. That's wonderful!

HENRY:

[before she can light up] Please, Stella, if you don't mind. Normally you know I don't care if people smoke, but I'm trying to air out the house.

STELLA:

[putting pack away] It's no problem. I need to cut back anyway. They just raised the price again. Inflation, you know—or just greed. So what's the occasion?

HENRY:

The occasion?

STELLA:

Yes. The airing of the house?

HENRY:

Hmm...I'm having to do it because of something Hollis McCreary did!

STELLA:

I was just about to ask where the poor dear is this morning?

HENRY:

He's out back. Out of sight at the moment.

STELLA:

Ha—that bad, huh?

HENRY:

Do you notice anything missing from this room?

STELLA:

[looking around at hardly a space unfilled] Well—it's hard to tell, really.

HENRY:

Then just think for a moment. It's quite obvious.

STELLA:

[looks around again as Henry stares at her] Well, I—

HENRY:

Instead of looking, just try and create a picture in your mind.

STELLA:

[suddenly startled] Ha! The cats—and dogs! Where did they all disappear to? I can't believe I'm missing twenty cats and two dogs!

HENRY:

Actually I brought down twenty-three cats this year. And they're all confined to the back porch along with Gentry and Ezra! While I was away yesterday, Hollis sprayed this entire downstairs with poison!

STELLA:

Poison?

HENRY:

Yes! He claimed there were fleas in his room! It was some kind of spray—the house was literally *reeking* with DDT! Now everything is contaminated and some of the cats are sick. I don't mind telling you that I came very close to asking him to leave—and I may yet! You know they've proved that stuff is deadly to birds.

STELLA:

I think it does something to the eggs.

HENRY:

It weakens the shells. People will sell you anything—even if they now for certain it will kill you!

STELLA:

Well, I buy very little; there's no need risking one's life unnecessarily I always say—ha.

HENRY:

It's just that I've got two Persian rugs I just recently bought thrown over the back fence trying to air them out in the sun. Who knows if that stuff will ever come out of rugs?

STELLA:

Well, I suppose poor Hollis must be feeling rather contrite this morning.

HENRY:

His explanation was that he was trying to do me a favor. I don't want unsolicited favors from anyone. But it's just too upsetting to even talk about!

STELLA:

Yes, I can see—

HENRY:

Yes. Well, let's just talk about something else. [begins to casually continue taking things out of the box] Tell me what you've been doing lately?

STELLA:

Oh, just the usual. I'm on my way home from the beach. It was getting rather crowded when I left. 'Tis the season, you know. The phonies are flocking in like gulls.

HENRY:

Hmm…there seems to be more and more every year.

STELLA:

Ha! Someday all that heavy luggage attached to pale New York faggots is going to sink this island.

HENRY:

[sly grin] Yes, but the irony is: their *haughtiness* will

probably keep all of them afloat!

STELLA:

[Throws her head back, she like a good hardy laugh.] How true! But that reminds me of a good one I heard out there this morning. There's this guy from Montreal—a ruddy-looking fellow named Mac—who has seriously announced that as soon as a large enough live shark is brought in he plans to buy the thing and water ski behind it all the way to Cuba. He's actually making a rig for it and has a group of fans already. What a character—there's some strange ones around nowadays, Henry.

HENRY:

How do you stand to associate with that crowd out there, Stella?

STELLA:

Well, it's the best place in town to get the early morning sun, dear. I like those gentle rays that don't require greasing myself up with smelly oils.

HENRY:

But I thought you worked in the mornings? Aren't you writing now?

STELLA:

[sighs] No, not really, except in my journal at fits and starts. I'm waiting to get a manuscript back but I don't know what I'll do with it next. A publisher in Chicago says I have a book but he won't touch it. It seems I've named too many names and for each of them he envisions a lawyer standing in his doorway.

HENRY:

Well—if it's a good story why can't you fictionalize the names? Everyone else does.

STELLA:

I don't think the book wouldn't stand up to that kind of a fix,
Henry.

HENRY:

Why not?

STELLA:

Well, most of the material is taken from my Hollywood
journals from years back.

HENRY:

[sly grin] Well, in that case, Stella, you should have nothing
to worry about—most of the names are probably fictional to
begin with.

STELLA:

Ha—that's a good point, dear. But I'm afraid it doesn't help.
The editor enjoyed the book immensely, but he doubts if I
can get it published anywhere. So—

HENRY:

Well, there must be something you can do? Maybe Tennessee
can suggest something?

STELLA:

He tells me in a roundabout way to chuck it—through bleary
eyes of course.

HENRY:

[slight reproach] Those bleary eyes have seen it all, darlin.'

STELLA:

Oh, I only meant he's incommunicable otherwise,
nowadays…you know…

HENRY:

Yes. But I think he's generally adverse to that sort of name naming, isn't he? He hasn't come out himself to the general public.

STELLA:

Well, he's untouchable of course. But I write what I know, Henry. I'm not an inventive writer of fiction. I record events going on around me and the real people involved. I'm simply doing what all good literary journalist do, making one's private world public—for the sake of the public, and good language, I hope. I'm at an age where I know without a doubt that one really hasn't anything to hide in this short life. I detest all this thinly disguised stuff going around today. It's not good writing, it's just a game, a guessing game of who's who. Just a lot of vomit in your ears.

HENRY:

Well, I think the threat of a lawsuit is a form of censorship, Stella. Did you tell your publisher that.

STELLA:

Henry, there are very few people anywhere who are able to tell publishers anything. As I said, I'm waiting for the manuscript back

.

HENRY:

Then what?

STELLA:

I'm not sure yet.

HENRY:

I would send it to someone else if I were you.

STELLA:

I'm a little fearful of the same response. I'm disappointed
of course. I wanted to throw a little reality out there and for
some reason I thought I had a right to. But I guess not. But—
well—I have to accept it. You know I've been circulating
manuscripts for years among friends. I think I've had readers
who count. Perhaps that's the limit of my success.

HENRY:

There's really nothing wrong with that, Stella. You're well
known in all the right places—you know that of course.

STELLA:

Well, I don't think of myself as a failure, Henry. Not at all.
I've lived a literary life. I can say that. The important thing
is that I'm not discouraged. I'm still interested in life and
want to write about it. *And* read about it. I may not have a
great mind but I think I at least have the ability to appreciate
great minds.

HENRY:

Yes, you're a—
 [Suddenly a series of short thumps come from upstairs, as
though someone is pounding on a wall.]

STELLA:

[looking up] What was that?

HENRY:

Just a minute… [leaves table and rushes halfway upstairs]
JACK! WHAT'S GOING ON IN THERE?

JACK'S VOICE:

It's all right. It's nothing, Henry.

HENRY:

WHAT WAS THAT POUNDING? I'VE GOT PAINTINGS
IN THAT ROOM!

JACK'S VOICE:

The paintings are okay, Henry. Don't worry.

HENRY:

I INSIST YOU TELL ME WHAT THAT POUNDING
WAS!

JACK'S VOICE:

I had a cramp in my foot. I had to hit it on the floor. It's okay
now.

HENRY:

I'VE NEVER HEARD OF SUCH A THING!

JACK'S VOICE:

I've had that problem since I was little. I have to hit my foot
against something until it goes away.

HENRY:

IT SOUNDED LIKE YOU WERE HITTING IT AGAINST
THE WALL TO ME!

JACK'S VOICE:

It just sounded that way maybe.

HENRY:

[calming down] Well, how much longer are you going to be
in there?

JACK'S VOICE:

Just a little while longer. Okay?

HENRY:

Very well. But no more of that pounding, please. I have company downstairs.

JACK'S VOICE:

Okay. I'm sorry, Henry.

STELLA:

[flatly, as HENRY returns to table] Well, who is Jack, dear? And what on earth?

HENRY:

Jack is a friend—a sailor. He's been staying with me for a couple of days.

STELLA:

It sounds a though he's having problems with his feet?

HENRY:

I don't know. I've never heard of such a thing. I'm not too sure that's what it really was...

STELLA:

What's he doing? His morning calisthenics?

HENRY:

Well, he likes to keep in shape. [sly grin]

STELLA:

One of those muscular types, huh?

HENRY:

No, not really. He's very, very average and very, very nice. He's from Nebraska.

STELLA:

Ah, yes. Away from it all. Uncontaminated…

HENRY:

Yes. There are so many smart-alecks around nowadays that it's wonderful to find someone who's just plain nice.

STELLA:

He sounds like a treasure.

HENRY:

Well, he only has a three-day shore liberty, so he's going back to his ship tomorrow. I shall hate to see him go.

STELLA:

I know the feeling, dear.

HENRY:

[removes a sketch pad from the box and leafs through it] Of course you never expect to see a sailor again. [Something in the sketchpad catches his eye.] Oh! I had completely forgotten about this! [admiring it] Well!

STELLA:

What? A drawing? Well, please let me see? I love even your rough work, you know.

HENRY:

[delighted with his find] One day in Miami I ran into two of the most adorable high school boys skipping school—and had them stand in a fountain wearing only their jeans. [holds it for her to see]

STELLA:

[squinting] Ah, such innocent expressions. It's *very* good, Henry.

HENRY:

Yes, I think so. I'd forgotten all about it.

STELLA:

I like the way they're leaning in against one another, too. Like two peas in a pod, you might say.

HENRY:

[studies it at arms length] Well, it's such a classic composition—the fountain rising above them in the background. I think I can definitely do something with it. I think I'll call it—*Baptism in Denim*!

STELLA:

Ha—perfect! I've always said you were as much a poet as a painter. But are you using models now? I thought your favorite subject was Alice?

HENRY:

The boys were just a spur of the moment thing. I'm not that fond of the human form, Stella. Just look at us: flat faces, long bony fingers—we're really rather comical as a whole. From an objective point of view even a barnyard mule has nicer lines and can be just as emotionally expressive.

STELLA:

I'm afraid I can't be that objective, dear.

HENRY:

Well, look at women—burdened with those permanently inflated bosoms.

STELLA:

[looking down at her large breasts] Well—

HENRY:

—A sure sign humanity's still in the suckling stage. [sly grin]

STELLA:

[glancing back down]: Ha! I just had a sudden vision—of humanity at my breasts.

HENRY:

Stella, honey, they're not *that* big!

STELLA:

Ha—no. But big enough.

HENRY:

Well, you've never had any complaints, I would say.

STELLA:

No—but then again they don't *guarantee* anything either. My friend Tony left them behind the other day.

HENRY:

The guy from San Francisco?

STELLA:

Yes. I think it was the first time I've ever lost out to a city. He said he could walk from one side of this town to the other in half an hour, yet he felt lost here. But he made the most dramatic departure: He kissed me goodbye and ran all the way to the bus station without looking back—three blocks.

HENRY:

Well, that's beating it out of town in a hurry.

STELLA:

Ha—in sandals no less. But he was sweet, a poet, and a beach lover also.

HENRY:
He was bisexual, wasn't he?

STELLA:
Yes, I think so—now! It's my fate, Henry. I can't seem to find a man who doesn't work both sides of the street.

HENRY:
[sly grin] Maybe it's because most of them do—

STELLA:
Ha! Sometimes I wonder. But—seriously, what is it about me do you think? –That attracts them?

HENRY:
Well, you're quite independent, Stella. You live and think like a man yourself.

STELLA:
Are you saying I'm manly, Henry?

HENRY:
No, far from it, I think. You're a very attractive woman— especially for your age. And you're very active and alive.

STELLA:
You're quite generous this morning, dear.

HENRY:
But did you ever have sex with a woman? You've never told me, I don't think.

STELLA:
Yes, once. I had to try it of course. But—I didn't get all

that much out of it. I've never felt the impulse to repeat the experience.

HENRY:
I think bisexuals are attracted to your openness, too, Stella.

STELLA:
Well, they're obviously not quite as open in return, let me say.

HENRY:
No, but they must feel that they can trust you. In the end you would understand. Wouldn't you?

STELLA:
Well, I have so far.

HENRY:
But, Stella, isn't the attraction somewhat mutual? It would have to be.

STELLA:
Well, I've always been drawn to men who are somewhat *sensitive*—Ha!—for lack of a better word.

HENRY:
Most of the bisexuals I know are married. Even the women. Doesn't that seem odd to you? On the surface it seems they should be the least likely to get married.

STELLA:
Well, unless it's two of the opposite sex. That would work quite well.

HENRY:
But that rarely happens—which is perhaps an even greater

oddity in a way. Don't you think?

STELLA:
In this case, the norm is what's odd.

HENRY:
Yes. Bisexuals prove that just because you prefer one thing it doesn't mean you automatically dislike the other. But I wouldn't want to be one myself.

STELLA:
Ha! I don't think you ever have to worry about that, dear. Nor I—

HENRY:
[sly grin] Well, perhaps they're the *true queers*—the rest of us are straight!

STELLA:
Ha!

HENRY:
But Stella—you seem never to have trouble finding a man, bisexual or not. I wonder why you don't find you somebody with a little money and get yourself off the road? I mean that in a nice way of course.

STELLA:
I can't say I haven't thought of that myself, Henry. But each time I try to image myself married, I somehow don't know how to act. I just can't imagine myself in that role. I can't see myself belonging to a man. And that's what it amounts to. I refuse to believe the gods made me incomplete. But that doesn't mean I've never loved—I have.

HENRY:

But you're not getting any younger, Stella. I'm talking about security.

STELLA:

My security has always been faith in myself, and thank God I still have that—as well as some beautiful enduring friendships. Lifelong friendships. Without those perhaps it would be different…

HENRY:

Yes, you do have a rare gift for that.

STELLA:

I think it's because I practice it. Friendship is like anything else; it takes practice. But what about you, Henry? I certainly don't think it's some sailor thumping around upstairs. What's your security? The money you're starting to make? I know you've had quite a few successful shows.

HENRY:

The money's just a means to an end. Security is simply a home, Stella. A home of my own—something I've wanted since childhood. But something also I can share.

STELLA:

I guess that's why you have two, then? This and your farm in Kentucky.

HENRY:

Yes, but the farmhouse isn't really livable in the wintertime. Just from spring until fall. It's mostly full of stuff I've collected for future use. But I needed it for Alice—and her descendents of course.

STELLA:

Lucky Alice. Then it's not one of those famous bluegrass horse farms with highfalutin names.

HENRY:

It's only seventeen acres, and I call it—Sweet Harmonica of the South!

STELLA:

Ha—I love it! How Henryesque. A harmonica-sized-farm. I can imagine you there with all your animals living in harmony until you're a hundred.

HENRY:

Yes, but obviously you haven't heard the latest, and you'll never guess—[sly grin]

STELLA:

I wouldn't even try.

HENRY:

I'm thinking of buying a house in Lexington soon. In the spring, I think. Providing I can make enough money for the down payment this winter.

STELLA:

My God, Henry—!

HENRY:

In fact, I have someone looking into it for me right now.

STELLA:

Are you playing monopoly now?

HENRY:

I was just walking around and I saw it one day. It's kind

of rundown a little, but it's in the old garden district of Lexington, within walking distance of downtown. And only about twenty minutes from the farm.

STELLA:
Well, it sounds like the perfect location.

HENRY:
What's perfect about it is the house itself. It's a three-story Victorian with rooms everywhere. With a garden in back. I knew I had to have it the moment I saw it. I really think it will make my life complete.

STELLA:
But Henry, three places! How in the world—!

HENRY:
[sly grin] I know it's going to cost me a lot of paintings.

STELLA:
I suppose so. My God, Henry, I wouldn't even want the responsibility of one house myself. I don't see how you transport everything back and forth as it is?

HENRY:
I'm really good at packing, you know. You wouldn't believe I can get everything in my old station wagon, including Alice, the dogs and cats, and still leave room for hitch hikers.

STELLA:
Well, that must be quite a sight, dear. But how does Alice take to hitch hikers?

HENRY:
She doesn't mind them at all. She sometimes spots them before I do.

STELLA:

I still don't see how you do it. I buy paperback thesauruses so that I can leave them behind.

HENRY:

I never leave anything behind—especially hitchhikers.

STELLA:

Ha—I've never had the privilege of picking up a hitchhiker myself.

HENRY:

You've never owned a car? Have you?

STELLA:

I've never even had a license to drive, Henry.

HENRY:

I wouldn't admit that to many people. They would lynch you in this society for that.

STELLA:

Ha—I've just never needed to drive. But I do like riding a lot. I've never really hitchhiked, but I've hitched a few rides you might say.

HENRY:

Well, where are you hitching to next—in the spring, I mean?

STELLA:

Oh, back up east I suppose, maybe hang out in the Village for the summer. And then—[HOLLIS appears in kitchen doorway already speaking: "Henry, some guy named Roger wants you out back." Steps just inside. Smiles at STELLA]

HENRY:

[going toward kitchen door] Roger who?

HOLLIS:

[shrugs] Just Roger. —Said you told him to come around sometime.

HENRY:

Well, just tell him I don't have time right now. I'm working.

ROGER'S VOICE:

[from the back steps] Henry! It's me, Roger.

HENRY:

[looking around the doorway, as HOLLIS and STELLA simply watch the action.] Don't open the screen door, Roger! The dogs will rush out. [sweet voice] Can you come back some other time? I'm kind of busy right now.

ROGER''S VOICE:

I'm on my break! You said anytime!

HENRY:

Well—okay. I'm coming. [to HOLLIS] Stay here and talk to Stella. [to STELLA] Excuse me, Stella. [He exits as HOLLIS advances into the room]

STELLA:

Well, how are you, Hollis?

HOLLIS:

Okay, I guess. You look nice this morning. That's a pretty dress.

STELLA:

Well, thank you, dear.

HOLLIS:

I didn't know you were here.

STELLA:

I just stopped by on my way home from the beach.

HOLLIS:

[sits down opposite her] Well, it's good to see you.

STELLA:

You, too. What have you been up to lately?

HOLLIS:

[looking dejected] Feeling bad, mostly. Did Henry tell you about the flea spray?

STELLA:

Oh, yes. Seems you've created quite a commotion.

HOLLIS:

Henry went wild on me over that. You should have seen him.

STELLA:

Yes, I can imagine.

HOLLIS:

I've been walking around on eggshells around him. He can really make you feel bad when he wants to. [gives her a sad smile]

STELLA:

Well, don't be glum. What can Stella do to help—within reason that is?

HOLLIS:

Within reason? Well—[looks down at the floor for a few seconds, then back up at her with a gleam in his eye]—I've always wanted to kiss you.

STELLA:

Always? I'm not so sure about that. But—if it will help.
[She leans forward and presents her lips. Hollis sits in disbelief for a second, then jerks forward to his feet to meet her lips. It is a solid, somewhat passionate kiss—only the touching is tentative. Finally she breaks it off, leans back and smiles.]
There. Feel any better?

HOLLIS:

 [backing to his seat] God, I thought you were kidding at first.

STELLA:

It was a nice kiss, dear.

HOLLIS:

Yeah. But it kind of makes you want another.

STELLA:

Ha! Not so fast—you're quite a bird dog, Hollis.

HOLLIS:

[smiles contentedly, confidently, leans back in his seat] So—have you heard anything back from Tony?

STELLA:

No, not as yet.

HOLLIS:

You think he's back in San Francisco by now?

STELLA:

I would think so.

HOLLIS:

Do you miss him?

STELLA:

Oh, I miss him some. It's nothing I lie awake over.

HOLLIS:

Anybody new on the horizon?

STELLA:

Ha—the only thing I've seen on the horizon lately is the sun, dear.

HOLLIS:

Well, what about around the corner then?

STELLA:

I'm always afraid of what I'll find around a corner, Hollis. But if you're trying to ask me if I'm looking for someone, the answer is no. I've got other things on my mind just now. There are other aspects to life, you know.

HOLLIS:

Yeah, I know. Life can get serious at times. That's why I'm glad you came by, Stella. I—I was planning on looking you up today anyway about something.

STELLA:

Yes?

HOLLIS:

Well, I don't know if it's within reason or not.

STELLA:

Oh?

HOLLIS:

It's kind of a real big favor.

STELLA:

How big?

HOLLIS:

It depends on how you look at it, I guess. But maybe—

STELLA:

I know I'm a fool—but say it quickly, just spit it out.

HOLLIS:

[quickly] Could you possibly put me up for a little while?

STELLA:

Put you up? Well, I'm sorry, Hollis. It just wouldn't be possible.

HOLLIS:

I've got enough money to buy my own eats and stuff, if that's what you're worried about.

STELLA:

No. It's my landlady I have to worry about. I'm sorry. This is over your spat with Henry, I suppose?

HOLLIS:

Stella, you don't know what it's like living here with all these damn cats! All my clothes smell like cat piss! I love Henry. I really do. I've never met anyone like him before. He's a true artist. But it's starting to get like the *Caine Mutiny* around here. You ought to hear some of the things he accuses me of.

Just a while ago he was going in and out of the back porch and let a kitten out, and guess who got blamed for it?

STELLA:
Well, I know Henry can be volatile at times. But one has to put up with the whims of one's host, you know. I can tell you that from long experience.

HOLLIS:
It's more than just *whims*! [looks toward stairs] You know what I had to do this morning? I had to beg this girl I know to go to bed with Jack, this sailor Henry's been keeping around. They're still up there right now in Henry's bedroom.

STELLA:
[looking toward stairs] Well, I had a feeling something was going on up there.

HOLLIS:
The guy got depressed or something and said he needed a woman because he misses his wife. So Henry charms me into getting Eva for him. I guess so he won't leave and go back to the ship—I don't know? But since the flea spray made some of the cats sick I felt obligated in a way. If you could just let me stay a couple a three weeks is all, until I can finish my screenplay, then I'm headed to California.

STELLA:
It sounds as though you're just having a lot of fun to me, Hollis. Both of you.

HOLLIS:
No, it's like Henry is turning into my step-father or something. It ain't no fun, man!

STELLA:

Well, you'll just have to believe me when I tell you that I can't take a chance on losing my own place. My landlady simply forbids overnight guests. But what about Eva upstairs? Is she the girl I've been seeing you with?

HOLLIS:

Where?

STELLA:

I saw you with a girl at the dock one evening. You had your arm around her and the two of you were standing there barefooted, oblivious to everything except the sunset, I believe.

HOLLIS:

Yeah. That was probably her. Why didn't you come over?

STELLA:

I just didn't. Doesn't she have a place?

HOLLIS:

No. She lives with her mother and sister. There's no way.

STELLA:

[Sighs] Well—If you really want to leave here that badly, let me check around town? Maybe I can come up with something.

HOLLIS:

I can't afford rent, you know.

STELLA:

No, I don't mean that. There's lots of guys down for the season. Lots of them hanging out at the beach in the mornings. Maybe I could connect you with someone who has an extra room or bed or something?

HOLLIS:

Well… I don't know. I don't want to be connected in *certain ways*, if you know what I mean?

STELLA:

Ha—I suppose you wouldn't have to worry about that, dear. It looks like you're pretty good at getting someone else to do your *whoring* for you.

HOLLIS:

[tries to chuckle this away] That's kind of hitting below the belt, Stella.

STELLA:

Is that where the truth hurts you most? Below the belt?

HOLLIS:

The truth is, Stella, sometimes you have to do things out of the need for raw survival.

STELLA:

Raw survival?

HOLLIS:

Yeah. Raw survival. Like Tom Wingfield in *The Glass Managerie* for example.

STELLA:

Ha—*Managerie!* I don't think your situation is quite as dire as that, dear.

HOLLIS:

No, but Henry going wild over flea spray and two cats out of two dozen getting sick isn't that dire either. There's always one or two sick cats anyway.

STELLA:

Well, maybe you just need to stay out of Henry's way for a few days, keep a low profile. Things will blow over. I can say one thing for sure about you, Hollis McCreary: You'll always come out landing on your feet!

HOLLIS:

[smiles proudly] Yeah. I usually do. It's in my blood.

STELLA:

In your blood? How so, dear?

HOLLIS:

Well—I don't like to brag, Stella. But I'm directly descended from General James McCreary, founder of McCreary County, Kentucky, who was appointed by President Washington himself to lead a brigade of militia against the Shawnee Indians. And on my mother's side I go back to Colonel Joseph Hayslett of the Second Confederate Calvary. So you see—

STELLA:

[Cutting in] Yes, I see—That would make you directly responsible for much of the fucking mess this country's in right now!

HOLLIS:

What fucking mess?

STELLA:

Hollis! You call yourself a writer and you don't know what's going on in this country?

HOLLIS:

Yeah, I know what's going on. I just thought you meant some

new mess or something. There's no television here to watch the news on.

STELLA:

That's all most of you southerners really want to do anyway, just watch and do nothing about it. It's *ingrained* in you, isn't it?

HOLLIS:

Stella. I'm for civil rights. God! It makes me mad that you think I'm not!

STELLA:

Well, I'm sorry. I guess we've never really talked about it. It's awful what's going on. The bombings, the burning…

HOLLIS:
Yeah, I know.

STELLA:

It seems it's the college students who are speaking up the loudest now. Doing the most to help. What about you? How really concerned are you?

HOLLIS:

Well, I'm concerned. I hope all this gets settled the right way, you know. But—to tell the truth—I'm just concerned with one thing mostly right now, Stella. I want to be a writer. That's why I quit school and came down here. All the greats have been here in Key West. I think there's inspiration here.

STELLA:

Yes, you're in good company here. There's no doubt about that.

HOLLIS:

[a little excited now] I know! When I first got here I went to see Hemingway's house and then Sloppy Joe's Bar. I wanted to sit down at the bar where Hemingway sat and have a drink.

STELLA:

Well, how was it? What you expected? Instant fame?

HOLLIS:

The bastards threw me out. When I didn't have an I.D.

STELLA:

Ha! That must have been devastating. But think of what a good story it makes, dear.

HOLLIS:

Yeah. But it kind of turned me against Hemingway.

STELLA:

Well, cheer up—it doesn't take much to do that nowadays. Although I loved him, too, growing up.

HOLLIS:

It just made me see who really matters. Tennessee, of course.

STELLA:

Oh?

HOLLIS:

I've read all of his plays since I've been here. He's my hero as a writer now.

STELLA:

Well, he's everybody's hero around here.

HOLLIS:

You mean everywhere! Just look at all he's done! He's raising the dead! He's bringing people back to life!

STELLA:

Yes…even though he's killing *himself* in the process…

HOLLIS:

What do you mean?

STELLA

I mean he's a great playwright, Hollis; but he also happens to be human—and therefore as vulnerable as anyone else, if not more so… I know him, I know him well. He's rarely sober nowadays—at least when I've seen him.

HOLLIS:

All great writers drink, Stella. It's their success as writers that matters. Whatever it takes to be the greatest?

STELLA:

Ha! Do you want to hear the truth about success, Hollis?

HOLLIS:

What is the truth?

STELLA:

Maintaining it, dear. One of those awful consequences build into the system.

HOLLIS:

But he is maintaining it. What about *Night of the Iguana*?

STELLA:

I don't think you realize how long a go that play was written. You're referring to the movie version, I'm sure.

HOLLIS:

Yeah, I guess so. But he's still the best.

STELLA:

Well, the world doesn't depend upon just one writer. Even a Tennessee Williams—who seems to be having problems of late.

HOLLIS:

You mean the drinking?

STELLA:

Well, that and a few other things—and maybe Edward Albee, let's say.

HOLLIS:

Who's Edward Albee?

STELLA:

Ha—I thought you knew what was going on in this country, Hollis?

HOLLIS:

Well, I don't know who Edward Albee is?

STELLA:

He's a new playwright. And he seems to have what it takes.

HOLLIS:

Is he as good as Tennessee?

STELLA:

Well, he's good let's say. But as good? Or even better? I'm afraid we won't know the outcome of that for sure for at least a hundred years, so it's a little too soon to say. And unfortunately, dear, I don't have that long to sit here and wait. I really must be going now.

HOLLIS:

No, Stella, don't leave. I love talking to you. Stay and tell me some more about Tennessee?

STELLA:

[picking up her bag] I do have to go. Get Henry to tell you some things. He's known him for a while.

HOLLIS:

He says he's going to take me over there but he never has.

STELLA:

Well, Tennessee's in and out quite often these days. Give Henry time; I'm sure he will.

HOLLIS:

I need to get back in good with Henry. Do you know the name of the blind man in the Bible? The one who kept bugging Jesus?

STELLA:

I know who you mean, I think. But I'm sorry I don't know the name. Why?

HOLLIS:

Henry needs it for a cat name. A kitten with one of its eyes out.

STELLA:

Well, Henry's very particular about names. They're kind of a consolation, I think. Can't you look it up?

HOLLIS:

The Bible's upstairs in his room. He won't let anyone go

up until they're through. That's why I'm saying it's like the *Caine Mutiny* around here.

STELLA:

[rising] Ha! Well, Hollis, I think you and Henry are a perfect match. But I really must go now. Tell Henry I'll see him again sometime.

HOLLIS:

[walking her to the door] Okay. You riding your bike this morning?

STELLA:

Oh, yes. It's the only sensible way to get around in this town.

HOLLIS:

[quickly] Can I kiss you goodbye?

STELLA:

[stops in doorway, sighs] Well, why not.

HOLLIS:

You're the most famous woman I've ever kissed.

STELLA:

Yes, I know.
[They embrace fully, a long deep kiss, but she parts from him as he reaches for one of her breasts]

HOLLIS:

What's the matter?

STELLA:

Just a kiss, dear.

HOLLIS:

But they're so tempting, Stella. Like big full moons.

STELLA:

Ha—yes, you'll always come out landing on your feet, Hollis McCreary, but mostly on someone's bedroom floor, I'm afraid.

HOLLIS:

That runs in the blood, too.

STELLA:

Yes, but fortunately for some of us it also passes through the heart. So long, dear. [She exits smiling]

HOLLIS:

[standing in doorway] I think I'm in love with you, Stella— Stella, Stella, for star.
[Her loud "Ha!" is heard as she goes off the porch. HOLLIS stands there watching her ride off on her bike as HENRY comes back in and returns to table.]

HENRY:

Stella's gone?

HOLLIS:

Yeah. She's just turning the corner on her bike. [turns toward HENRY] I like Stella. She's cool.

HENRY:

She's quite popular. She gets around…

HOLLIS:

How does she live?

HENRY:

[busy at table] Tennessee's helping her out this winter, I think.

HOLLIS:

He supports her?

HENRY:

He helps her out occasionally. They're old friends. He helps a lot of people.

HOLLIS:

He can afford it, I guess. Is she the Stella in *Streetcar*?

HENRY:

She's a New England belle, Hollis, not a southern one.

HOLLIS:

She's more like Maxine in *Iguana*… Are we still going over to his house sometime, Henry?

HENRY:

Yes, but I'll not take you like that. You'll have to wear a shirt and some shoes at least.

HOLLIS:

Don't worry. I'm saving some special clothes for that. My Sunday-go-to-meeting clothes.

HENRY:

I'm sure he'll appreciate it.

HOLLIS:

[goes over and plops down on couch] Well—did you do, Roger? I know that's what he wanted, wasn't it?

HENRY:

[sly grin] He was bursting at the seams, you might say.

HOLLIS:

Yeah, he did seem pretty anxious.

HENRY:

We did it behind the bushes beside the steps. That's why I let everything grow up in my yard. You never know when you'll need some privacy.

HOLLIS:

Did he have a big one? Like—[nods towards upstairs]

HENRY:

He was sort of average.

HOLLIS:

What? About six inches?

HENRY:

Not quite. But it's really how big around they are that counts. He was neither.

HOLLIS:

Can you tell by just looking? The way a person is built? How big they are?

HENRY:

Well, there are some general types where you kind of know. But there are a lot of exceptions, too. I don't try to guess, I just wait and see.

HOLLIS:

Well—let me ask you this: Would you rather have somebody good looking with a little one, or somebody ugly with a big one?

HENRY:

I don't care what it's attached to as long as it takes both hands to hold it. [sly grin]

HOLLIS:

But suppose you fell in love with someone with a little dick?

HENRY:

General cocksucking hasn't got a whole lot to do with love. You usually don't want the same one twice.

HOLLIS:
Why not?

HENRY:

I don't know. You just don't. It's the anticipation, I suppose.

HOLLIS:

Yeah, but *have* you ever loved anybody and stayed together?

HENRY:

Yes, once. He died.

HOLLIS:

I'm sorry.

HENRY:

You don't have to be.

HOLLIS:

Was that back in Kentucky?

HENRY:

No. It was in New York. But I did flee back to the hills to grieve.

HOLLIS:

Has he been the only one?

HENRY:

Yes, the only one. We were more than just lovers; we had a rare true friendship.

HOLLIS:

[after a moment] How come you never wanted to do me, Henry?

HENRY:

I didn't think you wanted to, did You? You were rather coy.

HOLLIS:

Well, I didn't really think about it one way or the other, I guess.

HENRY:

I know you too well, now. I can't do it with people I know.

HOLLIS:

Why is that?

HENRY:

It makes me feel self-conscious. It's just better with strangers.

HOLLIS:

What about Jack? He's no longer a stranger.

HENRY:

I'll probably never see him again once he ships out, so he's still like a stranger in a way. He'll be gone tomorrow.

HOLLIS:

[looking toward stairs with a scowl] I don't know—if you ask me it looks like he's abandon ship!

HENRY:

I don't think he's *abandoned* anything, Hollis. Give them a little while longer.

HOLLIS:

Yeah, that's just it with me: give somebody an inch and they take a mile!

HENRY:

He's giving her much more than an inch, Hollis. Believe me!

HOLLIS:

God, Henry! I didn't need to hear that—!

HENRY:

What do you want to hear?

HOLLIS:

I'd like to hear them come out of there for one thing.

HENRY:

Why in the world did you go along with this in the first place if it's going to cause you so much misery?

HOLLIS:

They've been up there over an hour now.

HENRY:

They could simply just be talking to each other too. I think Jack needed to talk to a woman as well. He's quite older than you; he may be a little more experienced with them than you.

HOLLIS

I may be young, Henry, but I've been around some—

HENRY:

Yes, I know how you've been around, Hollis. You go ahead of yourself loosening avalanches and setting deadfalls, then you innocently walk into them and start screaming *why me*! What are you going to do when something real comes along? Aren't you going to be confused?

HOLLIS:

I'm just trying to experience life. So I can write about it.

HENRY:

Then you need to learn something from your experiences and take more responsibility for how things turn out. You're creating an awful lot of negative emotion over this. I can feel it in the air, and quite frankly I don't like it. Don't you think you've contaminated this room enough?

HOLLIS:

I'm sorry, Henry. I really am. About the flea spray. I didn't think about it being poison.

HENRY:

Well, it is. Just don't do anything like that again without asking me. Animals are much more sensitive to chemicals than humans.

HOLLIS:

I don't think the cats are sick anymore.

HENRY:

I know; I looked at them before I came in just now. But Gentry and Ezra are bored. Maybe you can take them for a walk after lunch and give them some exercise.

HOLLIS:

Yeah. I hate to see them cooped up. I know it's my fault.

HENRY:

And did you move Alice? I didn't see her.

HOLLIS:

I put her in the shed. And gave her a little feed. Was that all right?

HENRY:

You didn't give her too much?

HOLLIS:

No, just a little, enough to get her to follow me in.

HENRY:

I shall need you to help me take her out to Boca Chica tomorrow after Jack leaves. The Cubans said to bring her anytime and I think she's ready. I'm just fearful that they may castrate the poor male and eat him before we can get there.

HOLLIS:

They eat them, don't they?

HENRY:

Yes. Everyday like we eat chickens.

HOLLIS:

I wonder if they know how famous Alice is? If they've ever read the Miami papers?

HENRY:

Probably not the arts section, anyway. But I wonder how she'll react to a Latin lover? A Cuban refugee, no less.

HOLLIS:

She's pretty-well swollen, so it shouldn't much matter to her, I don't think.

HENRY:

She won't mate with him if she doesn't like him. I don't care how much in heat she is.

HOLLIS:

We had a cow one time that jumped a six-foot fence and ran down the creek about two miles to get to this bull. That's wanting it pretty bad.

HENRY:

I think large female animals have orgasms, too.

HOLLIS:

I think hogs do. We used to raise hogs fer meat ever year. Sometimes we would keep a couple of sows over and breed them.

HENRY:

I'm not sure we should eat pig meat. I don't think we understand them as well as they understand us. It don't seem right.

HOLLIS:

I know I cried like a baby when we had to move to town and

couldn't keep them anymore. I loved them hogs. That was the biggest turning point in my life, I think, having to move to town.

HENRY:

Why'd ye have to move, Hollis?

HOLLIS:

My stepfather got hurt in the mines, so we had to move into town so he could work in a hardware store. Then after a while my mother got a job in a dress shop. God—that's when it all started...

HENRY:

What started?

HOLLIS:

The clothes thing. She got obsessed with clothes. And since we were from out in the county she thought we had to keep up appearances in town. She'd spend the last penny on clothes for everybody. Most of the time we had to skimp on things *unseen*—like food for instance—just to have better clothes than everybody else. She always told us kids that food just goes in one end and out the other, so what does it matter? We was raised on peanut butter and monogrammed sweaters...

HENRY:

Well, no wonder you missed the hogs.

HOLLIS:

All I know was that I never got enough to eat. That's why I'm kind of thin now. She drove everybody crazy with clothes, especially my stepfather. He drove a used Chevy but she dressed us for a Cadillac.

HENRY:

Well—one would never know it this morning.

HOLLIS:

How come? These? [looking at his cutoffs]

HENRY:

No. Why don't you take a good look at the bottoms of your feet?

HOLLIS:

[lifting one of his feet; the bottom is coal black]: Wow—man!

HENRY:

They certainly don't belong in a Cadillac. That has to be more than one day's accumulation.

HOLLIS:

Yeah, I need to go up and wash them, I guess. [looks toward stairs] —If they ever get through…

HENRY:

I just hope Eva's feet aren't that bad—she's in *my* bed.

HOLLIS:

She took a shower before she came over. That's why we took so long.

HENRY:

Good. It's been a while since I've had a woman in my bed. [sly grin]

HOLLIS:

Really? Did you ever have a woman in bed?

HENRY:

Yes, of course.

HOLLIS:

You mean you've done it with a woman?

HENRY:

[sly grin] Yes, once. Well, almost.

HOLLIS:

What do mean, almost?

HENRY:

I withdrew.

HOLLIS:

You withdrew? Why? Didn't you like it?

HENRY:

It felt like a glass full of fish worms to me.

HOLLIS:

[chuckling] A glass full of fish worms? That's weird, Henry.
I have to remember that. When was this?

HENRY:

When I was a teenager.

HOLLIS:

Yeah, but how did it come about? How did you get her?

HENRY:

It was when I was in the State Children's Home. One of the
older girls seduced me. I don't think she quite understood
why I liked to hang out with the girls.

HOLLIS:

What was the State Children's Home?

HENRY:

It was an orphanage in Louisville.

HOLLIS:

[amazed] You grew up in an orphanage, Henry?

HENRY:

Yes. Well—I was there off and on.

HOLLIS:

God—how come?

HENRY:

After my mother died. All us younger kids were sent there. I was about four then.

HOLLIS:

[with sympathy] Really? Wow, Henry. What was it like?

HENRY:

It was very ridged. Lining up all the time, staying in line. Especially when we had to line up to be chosen for foster homes and adoption. Mostly by tobacco farmers and their wives looking for farm hands.

HOLLIS:

Did you ever get chosen?

HENRY:

Yes, a few times. For foster homes. But I always got sent back to the orphanage after a few months. I just didn't fit in any place.

HOLLIS:

But what about your mother in Clay County? She's just your adoptive mother then?

HENRY:

Yes, that's where I stayed the longest, with a couple in Clay County. But I eventually got sent back from there too. [sly grin] I almost caused a mountain feud. But nobody got shot.

HOLLIS:

God, it's hard to imagine growing up like that…

HENRY:

That's just it—you need a good imagination.

HOLLIS:

Did you feel sorry for yourself a lot?

HENRY

Yes, at first I cried a lot because it was lonely. But we were all in the same boat. We were encouraged to be cheerful when people came around. Nobody wants to adopt a crybaby, they would tell us.

HOLLIS:

Well, do they still care about you? The people in Clay County?

HENRY:

Yes, that's where I go when I really want to go home. Although I never got along with the other people in the community. They just didn't like me.

HOLLIS:

I guess my problems were nothing compared to yours,

Henry.

HENRY:
Well, you're simply looking for a father figure, Hollis.

HOLLIS:
You think so?

HENRY:
It's obvious. It's quite classic too, you know, and biblical.

HOLLIS:
Everybody calls my father Big Daddy. Only he's not a rich plantation owner, but he's big. He sits on a bulldozer all day moving dirt around, and at night he goes out drinking and prowling for women. He does drive a Cadillac, but it's not a new one, a late model though.

HENRY:
Well, that must be how he gets the women.

HOLLIS:
Yeah. He lives in Corbin about forty miles away, but he doesn't want to have anything to do with us, my sister and me. We'd go for years without seeing him, so we got to calling him by his first name instead of dad. Forty miles is a long way to travel back in the hills.

HENRY:
Yes, it can be an eternity.

HOLLIS:
I ran away once and hitchhiked—but walked a lot of the way—to see him when I was about eleven, but he brought me back the same day and handed me a dollar when he let me out. He could be hard-hearted sometimes.

HENRY:

Sounds like he could be rather cheap too.

HOLLIS:

No, he was just trying to make a point, you know. My stepfather's the one that's cheap. He wouldn't give you a nickel. He had four kids by my mother—mostly on purpose.

HENRY:

Well—aren't you supposed to have them on purpose?

HOLLIS:

Yeah, but I meant he had a motive. My father and my stepfather were rivals for my mother. They fought over her a couple of times. Bloody fights, I heard. So when my stepfather finally got to marry her he had to out-do my father and have four kids. Kind of a way of wiping me and my sister out sort of. You know what I mean?

HENRY:

No. How does that *wipe you out?*

HOLLIS:

By outnumbering us.

HENRY:

Well, your mother obviously had something to do with it too, didn't she? Why would she—outnumber—her own children?

HOLLIS:

Oh, she was happy to have more kids. It gave her more paper dolls to hang clothes on. We weren't children; we were little store manikins.

HENRY:

Clothes are superficial, Hollis.

HOLLIS:

Well, that was really just a sideline thing. The biggest problem was her lying. She can tell a lie and then tell two more to back it up so you'll believe the first one. She makes you believe her, or want to believe her, and you do, thinking it's the truth this time, but it never is.

HENRY:

What does she lie about?

HOLLIS:

You name it. Whatever needs to be lied about. To get money. To get sympathy. To get you to do things. Like that time we had to move to town and I didn't want to go. I waited until they were all packed up, and then ran down to the creek bank and climbed up to the top of a tree. My stepfather came down and threatened me but that didn't work. Then they sent my favorite uncle down but I wouldn't come down for him either. I'd decided that after they all left I was going to go back in the hills and live. But finally here comes mommy. She had a picture of a bicycle she had torn out of a magazine. It was the new type that had just come out with the breaks on the handlebars. She promised me that bike as soon as we got to town. We'd go straight to the hardware store and get it. Well, after a while she wore me down and I said okay mommy I'm going to believe you one last time. When I came down she handed me that picture—and that's all I ever got—that picture. Later on I would get the picture out and show it to her to try and make her feel guilty but all she would do was laugh at it, like it was a big joke. It's hard being around her—cause you have to always be on guard. That's one of the reasons I left. She's like Tom Wingfield's mother in *Managerie*. Lives in her own world. And worries about money all the time.

HENRY:
Does she know where you are?

HOLLIS:
Nobody does really. I just told them I was going down to Florida for a while. I don't want anybody to know where I'm at. I want to feel free, totally free. Nobody to worry about but myself.

HENRY:
That's all right, but you need to at least write her and let her know where you are. That's not going to keep you from being free. I write my mother in Clay County all the time. That doesn't keep me from being free. It's the stupid people in the world who try to stop you from doing that!

HOLLIS:
I don't think *anybody* stops you, Henry.

[There is no answer to this except for a brief affirmative grin from HENRY as he picks up a pencil to make a note. HOLLIS uses this as an opportunity to turn and look toward the top of the stairs. When he turns back around he sits there quietly watching HENRY for a few seconds, then he casually looks down at one of his feet, looks back up again, then immediately back down again with concentrated curiosity] Guess what, Henry?

HENRY:
What?

HOLLIS:
A flea.

HENRY:

Where?

HOLLIS:

On my foot.

HENRY:

Are you sure it's a flea?

HOLLIS:

[leaning over closer to his foot] Yes, I'm positive. Right there.

HENRY:

Well, see if you can catch it and bring it here, I want to see.

HOLLIS:

[reaches down for it] Damn! It jumped!

HENRY:

Hmm…

HOLLIS:

[down on all fours looking for it] I swear it was a flea, Henry. Man…

HENRY:

It was probably a sand flea from your feet, Hollis. I wouldn't crawl around on that floor if I were you.

HOLLIS:

[intent on his search] It has to move again.
   [Suddenly a lighthearted voice calls from out back: Hennreee!—Hennreee!—Heennnreee!]

HENRY:

[going toward kitchen doorway] Who's out there?

VOICE:

[nearer, inside now] Andrew! Andrew coming through!
[ANDREW MAYHAN, mid-thirties, enters, dressed in
crisp tan slacks and a floral shirt, which is open at the collar
revealing a small round gold medallion on a thin gold chain.
He carries a drink in a clear plastic cup, which he will
occasionally sip from. He is a little high.]

ANDREW:

Henry! What in heavens name is going on, on your back
porch? I've never seen so many four-legged creatures
enclosed in one—[notices HOLLIS] Oh, and here's another.
[to HOLLIS who is starting to get up] Oh, please? Don't get
up! That's such a *lovely* position.

HOLLIS:

I was just looking—for something.

ANDREW:

Oh—well, look no further or farther, I'm here!

HENRY:

Andrew—did you close the screen door all the way shut?

ANDREW:

I can't be absolutely sure, Henry. There are two of them after
all.

HENRY:

Hmm…it's the outer one. [exits kitchen doorway in a rush]

ANDREW:

[coming over to HOLLIS, who is standing now] Henry

thinks I need no introduction. [extends hand] I'm Andrew.

HOLLIS:
[shaking hands] I'm Hollis.

ANDREW:
Hollis? Well, Hollis, how nice to meet you. I don't think I've ever known a Hollis before. How nice.

HOLLIS:
It's an old family name.

ANDREW:
Well, old families are nice, too. Where is yours from?

HOLLIS:
Kentucky.

ANDREW:
Well, that's where dear Henry is from. Then you must have come down with him this year?

HOLLIS:
[as HENRY comes back in] No, actually Henry and I met here in Key West.

ANDREW:
Oh, well that's possible, too.

HENRY:
[coming back to table] Hollis saw my Kentucky license plate and came running up to the car one day.

ANDREW:
Well—how poetic!

HENRY:

Yes. But what brings you around, Andrew? Do you have news or something?

ANDREW:

Of course, darling. Why do you think I've come traipsing through the back alleys of Key West to get to this phoneless outpost? Baby Doll herself will be pulling up in front of your house any minute now. We're all going to the beach!

HENRY:

Oh, he's back now?

ANDREW:

Yes. I know it's short notice, but it's not every morning we're offered such an event. And we're collecting people along the way as you can see.

HENRY:

Well, it's not the short notice. It's just that I can't go that far away from home today.

ANDREW:

Oh, Henry, you and your ominous horoscopes… We'll talk about you if you don't go.

HENRY:

I'm just too busy. I've got too much going on.

ANDREW:

But surely it can go on without you. We can't do without your spirited energy, and your outrageous antics that end up getting us all in trouble—like rushing us to the emergency room with an injured sea gull!

HENRY:

Isn't that what emergency rooms are for?

ANDREW:

But they're for *people*, Henry!

HENRY:

Hmm…not always.

ANDREW:

Heaven forbid any of us having to go back with a true injury. They would probably stand there and let us bleed to death!

HOLLIS:

[who has sat down on the couch] Are you all talking about Tennessee? Is he really coming?

ANDREW:

He's been known to, love. But just now he's getting *inflated*—his tires that is—two blocks over. [Festoons himself on the arm and back of the stuffed chair, so that as he turns from one to the other most of what he says is blurted toward the audience.] So you don't have much time to decide, Henry?

HENRY:

I've been trying to get to this for days. [indicating table] Besides I have to be here for someone who's leaving tomorrow. I can't just disappear.

ANDREW:

Who's leaving tomorrow? [mock frown] I hope it's not you, Hollis?

HOLLIS:

No—I hope not.

ANDREW:
Well, do you have someone hidden away, Henry? A hidden
trick?

HENRY:
[sly grin] Yes, but he's still in bed. My electronics technician
from the *USS Ranger*.

ANDREW:
Electronics technician? Well, I'm impressed. He must be very
intelligent. Does he have a high I.Q., Henry? *—Inclination
for queers?*

HENRY:
If measured by the inch he's a genius!

ANDREW:
My, my, I've never seen a smart prick before. No wonder
you have him hidden away. I can't wait to tell everyone that
they've missed Einstein's penis.

HENRY:
It's hard to miss, Andrew. [sly grin]

ANDREW:
Oh, I'm sure, Henry. It must be astronomical. [to HOLLIS]
Hollis, you're staying with Mister Faulkner too, I presume?

HOLLIS:
Yes. I'm just a guest though.

ANDREW:
Well, I can't help but notice that you bear a strong resemblance
to Degas—though not dressed as dashingly, perhaps. You
don't also paint?

HOLLIS:

[shaking his head] No.

ANDREW:

Oh, no, of course not. Painters don't put each other up—at least since Van Gogh and Gaugin. Is that not right, Henry?

HENRY:

Hollis is trying to write.

ANDREW:

Well, I should have known from those intense dark eyes. What are you working on, Hollis?

HOLLIS:

I'm finishing up a screenplay right now.

ANDREW:

A screenplay? Well, don't be surprised if they ask you to star in it also. You have very nice cheekbones. You would look fabulous on the big screen, you know.

HOLLIS:

[flattered] I just hope they take the screenplay.

ANDREW:

Well, so do I. I seriously mean that. But you are quite attractive, nevertheless.

HOLLIS:

[in the spirit of the moment] Well, so are you, Andrew.

ANDREW:

Oh, you don't have to say that—even though I probably am—am I not, Henry?

HENRY:

I've never known you to need anyone else's opinion on that, Andrew.

ANDREW:

True. But it has always been my bane. A beautiful face can be a real burden before it fades. You never know who or *what* is going to be attracted to your beauty.

HENRY:

Yes, but it usually promises more than it can deliver.

ANDREW:

Well, there you go being the philosopher again, Henry. [to HOLLIS, as if confidentially] Henry just doesn't realize that for the rest of us poor mortals the judgment of how attractive or unattractive we are is the most we can usually manage in life. They say that beauty is skin deep, but any good student of anatomy will tell you that it is principally a matter of bone structure—much closer to the soul than we had at first suspected.

HENRY:

How profound, Andrew.

ANDREW:

I was speaking to Hollis, who doesn't require profundity at such a tender age.

HENRY:

You never speak to anyone but yourself—everybody knows that!

ANDREW:

That's just not so, my friend. I haven't spoken to myself in years. Since I turned thirty as a matter of fact. Now the age difference is too great for me to have anything in common with myself. Now there's nothing to look forward to except— disappointment and—and resignation!

[A horn blows out front.]
Well! Speak of the devil and he arrives every time! [rises] What shall I tell them, Henry? We're kind of in a rush, you know. He's flying back out this evening.

HENRY:
Hmm…I want to speak to him at least. And give him a hug.

ANDREW:
[to HOLLIS as he crosses] You're welcome to come along too, Hollis. We're just going to camp it up. I'm quite sure someone of us can sit on your lap.

HENRY:
[leaving table] Hollis knows we can't leave just now. But he wants to meet Tennessee.

HOLLIS:
[rises, excited] Yes, of course!
[ANDREW stops abruptly near front door and picks up a figurine from a wall shelf. "Oh, This is new, isn't it? In a manner of speaking. Dresden?" Looks at the bottom of it. "Yes. Well, it's a wonder it hasn't been broken." He replaces it and goes out. HENRY stops to slightly readjust it before following him out. HOLLIS comes to the doorway and stops, looks out, then turns and rushes like mad into his bedroom. Momentarily a few thumps are heard and HOLLIS comes back out in a clean white shirt and his shorts, sporting shiny brown loafers and trying to get his leg into a pair of light-tan dress slacks. As he hops along he manages to get one leg in, then he suddenly trips and falls. He lies there holding his knee and gritting his teeth. At this point HENRY is heard calling

his name from out front. Hearing this, HOLLIS struggles to get up. It is the leg that is already inserted in the slacks that is hurt, so he hops over on his good leg to the arm of the stuffed chair to finish pulling them on. He hurriedly tucks in his shirt as he limps to the front door. HENRY is heard calling out in a sweet voice: "Have a nice time, you all." HOLLIS quickly limps out, waves and shouts: "Hi, Tennessee!" The horn sounds two short toots as if in response to this, and ANDREW shouts "Bye, Hollis!" as the car moves along. The horn blows again father away.

THE CURTIN FALLS

ACT TWO
[Just a moment later]

HENRY:
[as he re-enters, looking back at HOLLIS] I thought you were right behind me, Hollis? I tried to hold them but they were wild to go.

HOLLIS:
[stepping inside, looking disappointed] I got this crazy idea to change clothes. I didn't know they were going to take off so fast.

HENRY:
[crossing to table] Hmm… you can't expect America's greatest playwright to sit and wait while you change clothes, can you?

HOLLIS:
[limping back and forth trying to walk it off] No. I can't believe I did that.

HENRY:

Why are you limping?

HOLLIS:

I fell trying to get my pants on just now. [lifting his knee and flexing back and forth] It's okay now. That's really why I missed him. I fell.

HENRY:

Well, that's too bad. I can't help it if his free time and mine don't always conjunct. Besides, my astrologer told me not to go away from home today. That's where I was yesterday while you were spraying the house. She probably knew this was coming.

HOLLIS:

[taking a seat on the couch, rubbing his knee] Well, it must have happened for a reason. [sighs, resigned] At least I got to see him.

HENRY:

Yes, and he you. He blew his horn at you, I think.

HOLLIS:

[revived] Yeah. He blew his horn at me. Man…

HENRY:

And I'm sure Andrew is going on about you to the whole crowd right now. He seemed to be taken by you, you noticed.

HOLLIS:

Andrew's kind of nuts if you ask me.

HENRY:

Well, he's one of those nelly queens who gives the rest of us a bad name.

HOLLIS:

Who is he anyway?

HENRY:

His last name is Mayhan—one of those Palm Beach heirs worth ten fortunes the moment they slapped him on the ass.

HOLLIS:

He's *that* rich?

HENRY:

Yes. You probably missed your chance. He wouldn't be caught dead in a Cadillac.

HOLLIS:

Well, it would take more than a Cadillac…

HENRY:

He's been in-and-out, as they say. But when you're alone with him he cries and goes on about how miserable he is, or pretends he is.

HOLLIS:

How can you be miserable with all that money?

HENRY:

Oh, come now, Hollis. Hmm…

HOLLIS:

Well, why does Tennessee like him?

HENRY:

He's just part of the Miami crowd. I think Tennessee got drunk and had sex with him once. He's just play material now, if anything.

HOLLIS:

Play material?

HENRY:

He once told me most of his female characters are old queens he has known.

HOLLIS:

Tennessee told you that?

HENRY:

Yes.

HOLLIS:

Yeah, but his women characters are so real. You'd never know it.

HENRY

Well, why should you—women are women! I think you've been around this town long enough to know what I mean by that...

HOLLIS:

Yeah, I know. But that's except for *The Glass Managerie*, of course. That was his real mother and sister.

HENRY:

Yes. That was Miss Edwina and Rose.

HOLLIS:

I think that's my favorite. I've sort of modeled my screenplay after it—not the plot but the technique, the music. Only I use a Bob Dylan song for the background music.

HENRY:

That's all right. You have to begin by imitating those you admire.

HOLLIS:

I've almost finished it. A few more weeks, I think. I'd like you to read it since I wrote most of it here.

HENRY:

Maybe you can read it to me some evening and play all the parts. What's it called?

HOLLIS:

Heads or Tails? With a question mark. It's about why I decided to leave McCreary County.

HENRY:

I like the title.

HOLLIS:

The title comes from when I got down to my last fifty cent piece and decided to flip it.

HENRY:

How did you leave Kentucky on just fifty cents?

HOLLIS:

I—well, I sold some stuff, my college books and such. I just wanted to go off and write somewhere. And [shrugs] now I have a screenplay almost done.

HENRY:

So what do you plan to do with it?

HOLLIS:

Well, that's something I've been meaning to tell you. I think

I'm going to head out to California with it when it's finished.
I'm going to drop it off at some Hollywood agency, then I'm
going to head up to San Francisco from there.

HENRY:
Well, it sounds like you've been making some serious plans.
You didn't flip a coin, did you? [sly grin]

HOLLIS:
No. I've just been thinking about it here lately. It seems like
the next step for me.

HENRY:
I spent some time there once.

HOLLIS:
San Francisco? What's it like?

HENRY:
I loved the flowers—that's when I decided I wanted to come
back as a butterfly.

HOLLIS:
They say it's the *hip* place to be right now.

HENRY:
That's as good a reason as any—

HOLLIS:
I've already made some contacts out there—some people I
met up at the dock at Mallory Square one night. They were
giving me the lowdown on LSD. I think I want to go out
there and try it.

HENRY:
LSD?

HOLLIS:

It's an experimental drug, they said.

HENRY:

What kind of drug? Something like pot?

HOLLIS:

Yeah, it's something like it, only about ten thousand times stronger than pot. They said if you take it on Monday, you'll take it again before the week is out. It makes you hallucinate and think all kinds of amazing thoughts. You can blow flowers and colors out your mouth. [demonstrates by blowing his hands away from his mouth]

HENRY:

I do that every morning when I wake up.

HOLLIS:

It comes on little sugar cubes. A drop of it. That's why they say you *drop* it. You don't smoke it like pot.

HENRY:

Well, I've never smoked pot. But I know a lot of people who do. Stella does sometimes, I know.

HOLLIS:

She does?

HENRY:

Yes, but don't say anything about it.

HOLLIS:

I've smoked it twice myself. Eva got a joint of it from some Cubans girls she knows. We smoked it one day out at the beach. It was a kick, man. But then I saved half of it and smoked the rest of it one day back in my room a week or so ago. It was the day you went to Miami.

HENRY:

Hmm…I knew I smelt a trace of something when I got back. Like dried corn silk burning.

HOLLIS:

Yeah. That's what it kind of smells like. But, man—smoking it by myself was different! It's like a story that happens to you without you ever going anywhere. I only left the room once all day. And that was to go to the kitchen. But it seemed like it took forever to get there, like time slowed down and everything was in slow motion. And everything I looked at had some kind of *meaning*, like everything symbolized something else. Even a tiny broom straw on the floor seemed to signify something cosmic. And all the cats were walking around weird-like, watching me as though they could read my mind.

HENRY:

They simply knew something strange was going on in your mind.

HOLLIS:

But it was funny—after I got to the kitchen I forgot what I went after. I kept looking around and looking around for something, but I couldn't remember what!

HENRY:

Hmm…I know exactly what—that was the day you drank that whole quart of milk I had gotten for the big kittens. Wasn't it?

HOLLIS:

No, Henry. I swear! There was just a little bit left in that quart before you left. I ended up drinking a glass of apple juice. I know because I wanted something tart. My mouth was dry. In fact the empty glass is still in my room on the windowsill. There's no milk on it anywhere.

HENRY:
Well, why did you leave it there?

HOLLIS:
I just keep forgetting it, I guess. I'll get it though.

HENRY:
Make sure you do. I brought those glasses back from overseas.

HOLLIS:
Yeah, but something strange happened while I was on the pot was why I set it there. After I finished the juice and set the glass down, I glanced out the window and saw a car go by, and I thought it was an unmarked police car. I thought they were circling the block. Then I kind of panicked. I decided to go out back and hide in the shed where nobody could see me. But when I started out the door I changed my mind and decided to stay in my room and not answer the front door. I went back and sat on the bed, but then I changed my mind and started out again. But when I got to the door I changed my mind again and went back to the bed. It was weird. I must have done that four or five times. I wore myself out trying to make up my mind! It was all kind of psychological.

HENRY:
Why did you think it was the police?

HOLLIS:
[shrugs] I don't know. The car was going real slow and it seemed like the driver looked over here and sneered.

HENRY:

Well, I don't doubt that—some people have nothing better to do!

HOLLIS:

It was a black Ford. The police always drive black Fords.

HENRY:

Hmm…was it a *real* car, Hollis? Or was all this in your mind?

HOLLIS:

Yes, it was a real car. Only it didn't really come back again.

HENRY:

Well, I don't want the police around. I've had run-ins with them in this town before. They don't like me.

HOLLIS:

Well, it was just my imagination in a way, Henry. It was just the pot I smoked. After that I felt kind of tired and lay down on the bed and all these other strange images and thoughts kept running through my mind. I just lay there in bed and let my mind wander. I had some good thoughts.

HENRY:

Was there anything *insightful*?

HOLLIS:

I thought about how stupid my parents were, at first. How they were like children themselves, just muddling through life. That was kind of insightful. Then I had this long fantasy that seemed to go on forever about getting my screenplay made into a movie out in Hollywood—and going out with movie stars. It seemed real.

HENRY:

[sly grin] I love fantasies. Any particular movie star?

HOLLIS:

Yeah. Kim Novak. I realized it was her jaw that I liked most about her. The way her jaw is shaped. If I had my choice—

HENRY:

I think Stella knows her.

HOLLIS:

Really? God! Well…I thought about Stella a little, too. But you don't have to tell her that.

HENRY:

You mean sexually?

HOLLIS:

Yeah. I think I could get her.

HENRY:

The pot must have made you horny.

HOLLIS:

It did after a while. So I had to jack-off. But—it was strange.

HENRY:

Why was it strange? I assume you do that everyday.

HOLLIS:

Yeah, but it was real intense.

HENRY:

I suppose so. You had it in Kim Novak's jaw at the time. [sly grin]

HOLLIS:

I wasn't thinking about anybody. It was something I've never done before. It was weird.

HENRY:

You keep using that word weird that has no meaning to me. Everything is natural.

HOLLIS:

It wasn't something I naturally do. I tried to suck myself. Suck my own self. You know what I mean.

HENRY:

Well, that sounds more like desperation than weird—

HOLLIS:

I was just watching myself jack, like I was just a bystander or something, and I suddenly got this urge to suck it. I don't know why. I put my legs up over my head and bent my back and started pulling it toward my mouth with both hands. It was like about a foot away. So I kept bending my back more and more and the closer it got seemed like the more I wanted it. Finally I stuck out my tongue as far as it would go and kept stretching my neck until I finally touched it, flicked it with my tongue. But it was just for that one instant. I couldn't stay in that position because my back was hurting so bad, so I had to lay back flat to finish doing it. It must have been the pot. I never thought of doing anything like that before.

HENRY:

Well, to be honest I think you may be a little *latent*, Hollis. If you want to know the truth.

HOLLIS:

Latent? Really?

HENRY:

Yes. Doesn't it seem obvious?

HOLLIS:

I don't know…

HENRY:

Well, think about it.

HOLLIS:

You know anybody else that's ever done that before?

HENRY:

I saw a man at this little sidewalk café in Italy once who could lick the head of his like an ice cream cone while leaning over in his chair. He had his hat on the table so people could throw money in it. This was after hours of course, about two or three in the morning.

HOLLIS:

It must have been a doozy

HENRY:

Oh, it was unreal. Like he had pulled a black snake out of his britches.

HOLLIS:

If you're latent that just means you're latent, doesn't it? You can be just latent all your life can't you?

HENRY:

Yes, of course. You can repress it all your life.

HOLLIS:

It had to be the pot that made me do that.

HENRY:

What you did was rather overt, Hollis. Even though it was to yourself.

HOLLIS:

Well, you said I was self-absorbed.

HENRY:

Well, what further proof do you need? Did you do anything else?

HOLLIS:

I went to sleep after that.

HENRY:

I don't suppose there was much left *to do* after that?

HOLLIS:

Except when I woke up I thought it was morning. I had that dazed feeling, you know. So when I finally realized it was evening I ran up to the dock to watch the sunset. For some reason I just had to watch the sunset that evening.

HENRY:

Well, it makes for a good ending to your story, I suppose.

HOLLIS:

Yeah, but that wasn't the end. That's the same night I met those people from San Francisco. These two guys and two girls. All of them had real long hair, and they were all real soft spoken and friendly, like I had known them all my life. We just hit it off. But they were headed back the next day— said nothing was happening here.

HENRY:

Hmm…little do they know.

HOLLIS:

They called it *tripping* too. They said the effect lasted twelve hours; you can stay high and trip for twelve hours on one cube. If you take it on Monday you'll take it again before the week is out—one of the girls kept saying that.

HENRY:

My lord, Hollis! Aren't you afraid you may *swallow* yourself before the week is out?

HOLLIS:

But LSD is more of a spiritual thing, Henry. You're too busy seeing the universe to think about sex. They said some people even have out-of-body experiences. You get on some kind of cosmic plane. But then it can have a bad effect sometimes, they said. Sometimes it can turn into the worst nightmare you ever had and you can't escape. You just can't snap your fingers and come down. You have to wait until it runs its course. You can be out of your body and can't get back in... maybe.

HENRY:

Hmm...in that case you'd have to worry about what's ten thousand times worst than the police coming.

HOLLIS:

What's that?

HENRY:

The devil coming!

HOLLIS:

Well—maybe that's what I need, Henry—to see the devil coming.

HENRY:

You don't know what you're saying, Hollis.

HOLLIS:

I want to experience everything I can. I want to see for myself.

HENRY:

You don't have to experience everything first hand, you know.

HOLLIS:

I do. Because I've been lied to so much. I don't believe anybody.

HENRY:

That sounds egotistical for some reason.

HOLLIS:

I just want to experience things for myself.

HENRY:

Well, would you like to experience being beaten up all blooded and left for dead by a bunch of heatherns?

HOLLIS:

No.

HENRY:

Well, I have. It wasn't something I *wanted* to experience.

HOLLIS:

How did that happen?

HENRY:

Now how do you think?

HOLLIS:

Because of who you are? [HENRY doesn't answer.] When did this happen?

HENRY:

Never mind when it happened. It's happened more than once.

HOLLIS:

That's what's wrong with the world; there's people like that in it

.

HENRY:

Hmm…yes, and you can't expect the police to protect you from them either; the police are in with them!

HOLLIS:

I know. The police think they're God nowadays. This country's in a fucking mess, Henry.

HENRY:

More so than you realize, Hollis.

HOLLIS:

They're even talking about starting up the draft now.

HENRY:

Well, what will you do?

HOLLIS:

I don't know. I'll think of something. Act crazy, maybe.

HENRY:

One of the oldest tricks in the book, but it usually works. [sly grin]

HOLLIS:

You should be able to choose whether you want to go over there or not! This is a free country, ain't it? [chuckles]

HENRY:

That's the basic problem, Hollis. We've been made to think we're the only free country in the world. And everybody in America believes it. But it's not true, of course.

HOLLIS:

I guess that's part of what's wrong.

HENRY:

That's what I just said.

HOLLIS:

I think I could live anywhere in the world. I can't stand the thought of living an ordinary life. Just to go along with everybody else just because that's the thing to do, and you're afraid to do what you really want. Like I love being here in Key West. People don't seem to sweat the small stuff. I like being around homosexuals, too. I really like homosexuals. I never realized that before.

HENRY:

Why is that? [sly grin]

HOLLIS:

Well—they're more interesting than regular men.

HENRY:

Maybe it's simply because they flatter you, Hollis.

HOLLIS:

No, it's just that they're more free, more fun to talk to. And they've all read Oscar Wilde.

HENRY:

Yes, but you wouldn't want to be one yourself?

HOLLIS:

Maybe if I didn't like girls so much. But I'm not like everybody else; I don't look down on them.

HENRY:

Why do you think that is? That's the big question, you know.

HOLLIS:

The Bible, I guess. God destroyed Sodom and Gomorra.

HENRY:

Well, not all homosexuals are nice. The Sodom and Gomorra types were not very hospitable, you know.

HOLLIS:

Still, everybody lumps them together.

HENRY:

It isn't really Sodom and Gomorra anyway, Hollis. It has nothing to do with religion, or all that other stuff. The reason is just simply a deep-seated jealously—which turns into hate.

HOLLIS:

You mean people hate homosexuals because they're jealous of them?

HENRY:

Yes, subconsciously. All that other stuff has been just a conscious effort down through the ages to keep it subconscious.

HOLLIS:

But why would they be subconsciously jealous?

HENRY:

You tell me, Hollis. [sly grin] Figure it out.

[JACK FARLY, an average looking man in his mid-twenties, appears in the upstairs doorway wearing only white boxer shorts. He furtively looks down at them then quickly goes back in. But HENRY senses his presence.] Jack!

JACK:

[reappearing, looking anxious] What, Henry?

HENRY:

[going toward stairs] Are you all about finished? Are you coming down?

JACK:

Yes, we're getting dressed.

HENRY:

Well, I think Hollis is waiting to take her home.

JACK:

Hold on! [leans back inside to listen] She said she had to go to the bathroom.

HENRY:

Oh. Well, all right. [JACK goes back in without a word.]

HOLLIS:

Well, it's about time.

HENRY:

What time is it?

HOLLIS:
[heavily] It's after ten, Henry.

HENRY:
Well, I think I'll go out and check on Alice while we're waiting.

HOLLIS:
She was okay. I left her in the shed.

HENRY:
I need some fresh air. I still get a whiff of that stuff occasionally. I only hope I can let the animals out this evening.

HOLLIS:
It should be okay by then. It's been twenty-four hours.

[HENRY exits. HOLLIS sits there a moment more looking toward the stairs, then he rises and wanders over to HENRY'S table; after snooping around for a few seconds, he turns and goes into his bedroom. He soon returns wearing a straw Panama hat to match his slacks, and looks rather dapper now. He stands at the foot of the stairs looking up. Finally he goes on up but stops near the top, deciding whether to go on in or not. At this instant HENRY strides back in, but when he sees HOLLIS he seems to stiffen in his tracks.]

HENRY:
HOLLIS! COME DOWN FROM THERE!

HOLLIS:
[as he begins to descend stairs] But they're through, Henry.

HENRY:
I'M NOT TALKING ABOUT THAT!

HOLLIS:

What?

HENRY:

YOU KNOW EXACTLY WHAT! I JUST EXAMINED ALICE!

HOLLIS:

Examined Alice?

HENRY:

YES! HER VAGINA!

HOLLIS:

What about it?

HENRY:

YOU *RELIEVED* YOURSELF IN HER, HOLLIS!

HOLLIS:

Relieved myself?

HENRY:

YES! It was quite obvious! I had to wipe her with a rag!

HOLLIS:

All I done was put her in the shed, Henry.

HENRY:

That was so you couldn't be seen!

HOLLIS:

I don't know what you're talking about? I never touched Alice. I swear.

HENRY:

THAT'S A LIE!

HOLLIS:

No, it ain't, Henry. It's the truth. I just fed her and give her some water.

HENRY:

THE TRUTH AIN'T IN YOU! NOW I WANT YOU TO PACK YOUR THINGS AND GO! RIGHT—THIS— MINUTE!

HOLLIS:

Go? You mean leave?

HENRY:

You heard me!

HOLLIS:

[shrugs] If that's what ye want, Henry, okay! [entering his bedroom] Just give me a chance, I'll pack up.

HENRY:

[standing in doorway, looking in] That's why you give her that extry grain – to get her to stand still fer ye!

HOLLIS:

[from bedroom] I give her that extry feed cause she was hungry. I didn't *relieve* myself in her, as you say.

HENRY:

THAT'S A BLACK LIE, HOLLIS.

HOLLIS:

No, that aint no *black* lie, Henry.

HENRY:

You deny everything you do; that's yore main problem, Hollis! [points] That's my towel, by the way.

HOLLIS:

I'm just pickin it up out of the way.

HENRY:

Just leave it yonder on the bed. They aint no need to fold all that stuff – it all looks dirty anyways.

HOLLIS:

I'm doing it as fast as I can, Henry. But that was just natural discharge coming out of Alice, cause she's in heat.

HENRY:

I think I know the difference, Hollis. They aint nothing so distinct as DRIED SEMEN!

HOLLIS:

I've got a girlfriend, Henry! Why would I do that?

HENRY:

Yes, why? If they's one thing I know about you, Hollis, it's that yore capable of *anything*!

HOLLIS:

I ain't capable of fuckin NO GOAT!

HENRY:

DON'T GET SMART!

HOLLIS:

I ain't getting smart. I'm just saying goats er too hi-strung—
!

HENRY:

You should know! I may have to take her to the vet over this.

HOLLIS:

Well, do what ye have to do, Henry.

HENRY:

Just be lucky I don't call the law. What you did is agin the law in Florida.

HOLLIS:

You shore you want to drag Alice's name through the mud?

HENRY:

THAT'S IT! [stomps his foot] JUST STUFF THE REST IN THERE AND GET OUT!

HOLLIS:

OKAY! I'm trying to—! I got a toothbrush upstairs…

HENRY:

Just forget that!

HOLLIS:

All right, have it yore way. You always do!

HENRY:

[stepping back from doorway] It's my house! Now! That's all ye come with. Please *leave*!

HOLLIS:

[entering with a large duffel bag over his shoulder] This ain't *all* I come with, Henry! [stops at foot of stairs and calls up] EVA! [waits but there is no answer] EEVA!

HENRY:

She's still in the bathroom. I'll send her when she comes down.

HOLLIS:

No! EEEVA!

HENRY:

You can wait on her outside, Hollis! I insist!

HOLLIS:

No. I ain't leaving her!

HENRY:

I don't care! [points toward front door] Outside! I want you outside right this MINUTE!

HOLLIS:

[calls upstairs] EVA! WHAT'S TAKIN YE SO DAMN LONG? COME OWN!

HENRY:

ALL RIGHT! THAT'S IT! I'M GOIN DOWN THE STREET AND CALL THE LAW! YOU'LL *SEE* WHAT I CAN DO! [starts out]

HOLLIS:

Okay, I'll go! If that's the way ye wont it. I'll wait on her out in the street.

HENRY:

No! I want you clean out of the neighborhood now!

HOLLIS:

Well, I'll be up yonder on the corner then. How's that?

HENRY:

No! Out my sight, Hollis! I mean it! Just keep going up the street. And don't look back!

HOLLIS:

God, Henry!

HENRY:

GO! Before I go call the law!

HOLLIS:

[takes a last look upstairs] Just tell her to meet me up at the dock. Can ye do that?

HENRY:

Yes. Leave now, Hollis!

HOLLIS:

[as he exits in a huff] I think I'll just go on to Californya.

HENRY:

That's a good idea.

HOLLIS:

I'll send ye a postcard, Henry.

HENRY:

Fine.

HOLLIS:

[going off the porch] So long, Key West!

[HENRY returns to the table and leans toward the window, taking several deep breaths through his nose to calm himself. EVA LIMING appears at the top of the stairs and descends a few steps. She is a pretty, slightly plump "girl" of twenty, wearing a halter-top and shorts. She looks flushed and is touching her neck with her finger tips as though it is tender.]

EVA:

[softly] What's going on? I was afraid to come down.

HENRY:

[turning toward stairs] I'm sorry you were frightened.

EVA:

What happened? Where's Hollis?

HENRY:

He's on his way to Mallory Square. If you hurry you may catch

EVA:

[puzzled] What's he going to Mallory Square for?

HENRY:

I don't know how much of that you heard up there, but Hollis doesn't live here anymore.

EVA:

I don't understand?

HENRY:

I simply had to ask him to leave.

EVA:

Leave?

HENRY:

Yes. —To not come back.

EVA:

[descending stairs in disbelief] You mean Hollis isn't coming back here?

HENRY:

No. He took all his belongings with him.

EVA:

You must be kidding.

HENRY:

No. I'm sorry. I'm not.

EVA:

I can't believe this!

HENRY:

Look over there in his room if you want. All his stuff is gone.

EVA:

[goes to bedroom door and looks in] He's gone. He's really gone.
[turns back to Henry] Why? What happened?

HENRY:

I don't think I want to go into that—

EVA:

I think I deserve to know.

HENRY:

It wouldn't help you in the least to know. Believe me.

EVA:

Well, was it *me*? Was it over *this?* [glances upstairs]

HENRY:

No. It was something else entirely. Have Hollis tell you if you really want to know.

EVA:

[looks around as if dazed] You mean that I—I did this for *nothing*?

HENRY:

No, not for nothing. I wouldn't say that—

EVA:

I feel stupid! Really stupid! I can't believe this? He just left me here like a piece of *crap?*

HENRY:

[sympathetic] It couldn't be helped. So please don't—well, try not to get too upset about it, darlin.'

EVA:

Well, how else am I supposed to get—except—upset…

HENRY:

I think you really need to see Hollis about this. Like I said, he's going to the dock to wait for you.

EVA:

Well, he can just wait there forever as far as I'm concerned. I don't think I ever want to see him again.

HENRY:

You may feel better after you've talked to him. It may not be as bad as it seems.

EVA:

That's easy for you to say. You ain't spent two hours up there with that guy that ain't even shaved! My face is burning off.

HENRY:

Yes, I can see that. Can I get you some lotion?

EVA:

I found some in the bathroom already.

HENRY:

Well, is there anything else I can do?

EVA:

Yes, you can tell me something.

HENRY:

Tell you what?

EVA:

What Hollis said about me?

HENRY:

Said about you when, dear?

EVA:

—While I was upstairs.

HENRY:

Well—he didn't say much. He was mostly concerned because he thought you all were taking too long, wondering when you were going to be through.

EVA:

Was that all?

HENRY:

Yes, just waiting for it to be over, mostly.

EVA:

—Over, huh? Well, it's over—if that's what you want to call it. That's a relief anyway—not having to go all the way through with it, I guess. Even though I can't help feeling sorry for him now. [glances upstairs]

HENRY:

Oh? Why do you say that?

EVA:

He didn't have no cramp in his foot; he was hitting the wall above the bed with his fists cause he couldn't do anything.

HENRY:

I thought there was something more to that.

EVA:

That's what that pounding really was. I thought he was going to go nuts.

HENRY:

He couldn't perform at all, then? Is that what you're saying?

EVA:

About the only thing he did was beard me to death.

HENRY:

I'm sorry. He needed to have gotten up and shaved at the least.

EVA:

I was ready to leave after a while, but he kept begging me to stay. He almost started crying once, so I felt sorry for him. He even [glances upstairs] went outside the door and looked through the keyhole at me to try and excite himself. You talk about desperate—

HENRY:
Yes. Well, I want to thank you for doing this. And if there's anything I can do for you, I'll gladly repay you in some way. But not with money.

EVA:
I don't want no money. I'm not a whore. I only did this for Hollis, you know. He came over and got me out of bed. I wasn't even hardly awake yet. He talked it up like it would make our relationship better and all. But I didn't go for that. Then he started begging: Do it for me; do it because you love me and because I love you? Do just this one thing, just this one thing for me? I was hoping it was not really true when I got here. He claimed Jack was your best friend. But he's really just some sailor passing through. I found that out.

HENRY:
I've only known him for a couple of days. But I've found him to be extremely nice. The point is, I think he needed a woman very badly.

EVA:
Why couldn't he go up town to one of the bars and pick somebody up? Why couldn't he get his own girl?

HENRY:
Well, it was kind of too early in the morning for that, I think. Besides, I'm very sure he's shy around women.

EVA:
So Hollis just volunteers me for this?

HENRY:

He said you might be willing to do it. So I suggested he ask you. I don't know much about yourall's relationship. I only know what Hollis tells me. I'm not sure if he's always truthful. I ran into Hollis on the street, you know. Out of the blue. I was told I would meet someone I would remember for the rest of my life that day. And—

EVA:

[cutting in] I could tell you a few things about him you probably don't know.

HENRY:

I wouldn't doubt if he's not wanted by the police somewhere.

EVA:

You guessed it.

HENRY:

I thought so. What was it?

EVA:

I'll just leave it at that—

HENRY:

Well, why bring it up if you're not going to tell me? [sly grin]

EVA:

He forged some checks back in his hometown. They're still after him he says.

HENRY:

Well, that doesn't surprise me. Maybe that's why he's so anxious to take off for California?

EVA:

[Stung] He's going to California?

HENRY:

Yes. But—I see you didn't know?

EVA:

No. Are you sure?

HENRY:

That's what he said

EVA:

When?

HENRY:

As far as I know he's leaving today.

EVA:

Well—I guess that's that—[getting choked up] He's leaving. And he's played this awful joke on me. [shakes her head slowly, tearfully] I don't know what to do now...

HENRY:

You need to go up to the square and talk to him?

EVA:

Why?

HENRY:

[soothingly] He wanted you to come there.

EVA:

He just wants to break it off with me. I love Hollis. I just wish he loved me. Who else would do what I did just because he wanted me to? [wipes her tears away]

HENRY:

I think you need to be saying this to him. Why don't you go meet him and try and persuade him to take you along.

EVA:

If he'd wanted me to go, he'd a told me, don't you think?

HENRY:

Well, I don't think he was expecting to go this soon. So he may have been going to tell you—one way or the other.

EVA:

By that you mean he hadn't made up his mind about me? Going.

HENRY:

I don't know. But he may think it's to his advantage to take you along.

EVA:

Why?

HENRY:

For one thing, he knows you'll do anything for him now.

EVA:

I won't do that up there again. You can bet.

HENRY:

He doesn't need to know that—does he? [sly grin]

EVA:

I don't think I would even want to go with him thinking that.

HENRY:

Well, it sounds as if you two have a lot to talk about then. He's probably there by now.

EVA:

I guess I'll go then. [moves toward front door]

HENRY:

Yes, good luck now.

EVA:

[slowing near doorway] Yeah, thanks. By the way—I liked all your paintings up there. I wanted to tell you that.

HENRY:

Thank you. I put them there to dry and to store them. Most of those will be in my next show.

EVA:

[stopping, as if for a second] They're really nice.

HENRY:

Yes.

EVA:

But there's one up there I didn't get? The one with the apple tree and purple sky? It's got little fish hiding in among the apples. Why is that?

HENRY:

[coming around from table] That one's called *Adam and Evening*.

EVA:

Adam and Evening? Like in the Garden of Eden?

HENRY:

The little fish didn't remind you of anything? [sly grin]

EVA:

I don't know. Just little fish with big smiles on their faces. God knows I spent enough time looking at them.

HENRY:

They're symbols, dear. For penises.

EVA:

Penises?

HENRY:

Yes. I put them in among the apples to tempt Adam. While Eve was away.

EVA:

But why?

HENRY:

Well, do you know anything, anything at all on God's green earth that provides more pleasure?

EVA:

I guess I never really thought about it. [forces a chuckle] So long. [She rushes out.]
[HENRY walks to doorway and watches her go off the porch, then goes over to the foot of the stairs and calls up] JACK? [ascends a few steps and calls again] JACK, ARE YOU COMING DOWN?]

JACK:

[from upstairs] Yes. Just a moment, Henry.

HENRY:

[sweet voice] Why don't you go for a walk and get some air

[There is no answer to this, so Henry crosses back to table and resumes his work. After a moment JACK appears at the top of stairs, dressed in navy whites, carrying a small blue duffel bag in his right hand that should be hidden from HENRY at first. He descends a few steps and looks around the room. HENRY becomes aware of him and turns towards the stairs.]
Oh—you're all dressed. And shaved, I see.

JACK:

[looking around nervously] Yeah, a quick shave. What happened? Was Hollis upset?

HENRY:

It was nothing—nothing to do with you. Come on down. They're both gone.

JACK:

[relieved] They're gone? [descends stairs]

HENRY:

They won't be back. Are you all right?

JACK:

 [sighs] I'm okay, I guess.

HENRY:

You should go out for a walk and get some sun. It's a beautiful day—a sin not to take advantage of it. [sees duffel bag] Well, what's that? [alarmed] Hmm…are you leaving?

JACK:

Henry…I think I'll go on back to the ship.

HENRY:

Oh?

JACK:

I need to get my gear and everything stowed away.

HENRY:

I thought you would have plenty of time to do that tomorrow?

JACK:

Well, there's laundry and other things I forgot I had to do. [goes toward Henry] I just want to shake hands and—

HENRY:

I don't want to shake hands. Why are you leaving, Jack? You couldn't be in that big of a hurry?

JACK:

I just want to say goodbye and go, Henry. Okay?

HENRY:

Jack. I went to a lot of trouble to get Eva for you, you know.

JACK:

I know. I'm sorry. Don't be hurt.

HENRY:

You can't hurt me, Jack. But you can give me an explanation.

JACK:

There's no explanation. I just feel I need to get back to the ship.

HENRY:

Are you going because of Eva? She told me what happened up there.

JACK:

She did?

HENRY:

Yes, everything. About why you were pounding on the wall. Everything.

JACK:

I'm sorry about that. I just—lost it for a moment. That's never happened to me before.

HENRY:

Well, it happens sometimes.

JACK:

I couldn't understand it. The more I tried—[shrugs]

HENRY:

—The worse it got. You were just too conscious of it, that's all.

JACK:

It's just never happened to me before. Not being able to—

HENRY:

Hmm…not even with your wife?

JACK:

No. I've never had that problem with my wife.

HENRY:

Do you really have a wife, Jack?

JACK:

Yes. Why would I lie about that?

HENRY:

No wedding ring for one thing…

JACK:

I'm in electronics, remember? It's not safe to wear jewelry. I don't usually wear it unless I'm home. [sets the bag down and takes out his wallet, goes over to HENRY and holds picture section out to him.] I not only have a wife…

HENRY:

[cocks his head to look] Hmm…well…you've been busy I see. You didn't mention you have children, too?

JACK:

I know. I just didn't. That was taken last summer. [puts wallet away]

HENRY:

I wonder how you support them all on a sailor's pay?

JACK:

It's not easy. I had to send extra money home when we docked. I guess if I hadn't run into you I'd had to stay aboard all this time.

HENRY:

So why are you in such a hurry to go back aboard?

JACK:

It's just time to go, that's all. Like I said, I've a lot to do.

HENRY:

You're beginning to sound a whole lot like you did this

morning when you woke up missing your wife.

JACK:

How was that?

HENRY:

Fishy.

JACK:

Oh…

HENRY:

Why don't you sit down, Jack? You look like you need to.

[JACK is standing by the stuffed chair and involuntarily drops down in it as though he is weary, and begins rubbing his forehead as if to relieve tension.]
I don't think you're telling me the real reason you want to go back. It must have something to do with what happened upstairs. So why won't you tell me?

JACK:

[sits with his elbows resting on his knees, one hand tucked into the other, staring intensely at the floor.] I… [shakes his head negatively]

HENRY:

Please, Jack! I can't stand this evasiveness. Either say something or go ahead and leave!

JACK:

I'm—trying to, Henry, ….

HENRY:

Very well.

JACK:

It's hard to explain. I just feel…

HENRY:

What?

JACK:

I'm afraid…

HENRY:

You're afraid? —Of what, Jack?

JACK:

[tears starting to well up] Don't you know?

HENRY:

Hmm… I think I'm beginning to—

JACK:

[wiping his eyes with a shaky hand] I've never actually stayed like this before…with anyone…

HENRY:

Yes, that was obvious.

JACK:

You know…it's always been just a quick blowjob somewhere…and kind of forget about it five minutes later…

HENRY:

—Until last night. Is that it?

JACK:

Yes…[His hands are beginning to shake.]

HENRY:

So that's the reason for Eva? To try and erase that? That's incredible, Jack!

JACK:

Henry, I—[Suddenly his hands begin to shake vigorously, uncontrollably. He looks down at them in horror and disbelief.]

HENRY:

What's happening to you, Jack?

JACK:

[looks up at Henry and sobs] God, I don't know—

HENRY:

[comes around from table and grabs Jack's hands and holds them steady] Jack! Stop it! What are you doing to yourself?

JACK:

I can't—help it!

HENRY:

Yes, you can! Stop it! You're just being psychosomatic! [releases Jack's hands and they slowly stop shaking.] Now calm yourself. Please!

JACK:

I'm sorry. [looks at his hands, turns them over, as if they were now something autonomous] I don't know what happened...?

HENRY:

Fear! Common fear! I've never seen anyone *fear* it so much!

JACK:

[places his hands on his knees and grips them, looks stunned]
I don't know what happened to me—

HENRY:

Hmm…it was simply mind-over-matter. It's what happened with Eva, too, technically. Are you going to be all right now?

JACK:

I felt my mind shaking too, Henry.

HENRY:

I can't understand how you worked yourself into this?

JACK:

I went too far…

HENRY:

You simply reciprocated last night.

JACK:

Reciprocate? That makes it sound—different…

HENRY:

That makes it sound abstract and far away, doesn't it? Well— you sucked me for a few seconds last night, Jack. It wasn't for long, but it may have been long enough—

JACK:

Long enough for what?

HENRY:

Long enough to make you think you may want to do it again. That's what this is all about, isn't it?

JACK:

Something like that I guess…

HENRY:

You did it on your own. Suddenly without warning as I recall. I was nearly asleep by then; you must have lain awake thinking about it? Then you woke up this morning acting strange.

JACK:

I had a dream this morning before I woke up. I dreamed I was being court-martialed but nobody would tell me why.

HENRY:

Well, I guess you know why now.

JACK:

Yes…

HENRY:

This couldn't have come as that big a surprise to you, Jack. Didn't you think this would happen sooner or later?

JACK:

No. I've just always been the—straight person. You know…

HENRY:

Well, sometimes the straight person starts to bend a little.

JACK:

I've never reciprocated before. I worked in the supermarket back home and the assistant manager used to blow me back in the back after we closed up. And then I got married a couple of years later and didn't really think about anything like that again. I come from a very religious family and my wife was religious, so I kind of got back in the church for a while. I still go to Mass sometimes.

HENRY:

So when did you start again? When you joined the navy?

JACK:

[slowly] Yeah. I thought I was doing the right thing joining the navy. I wanted to go to electronics school. But then I started getting back into that—It started with me and this buddy of mine. We were on our first cruise. When we docked most of the guys hit the bars and started picking up prostitutes. But me and my buddy were both married, so we figured that kind of thing was out for us. But one night before we shipped out we were sitting in this little café drinking beer, and this guy at the next table started buying us rounds. I guess we got a little high and one thing led to another and we ended up letting him blow us in the alley behind the place. After that we sort of looked for people each time we came into port. We learned where to hang out at the right places. That's how it all got started again.

HENRY:

Did you and your buddy ever do anything with each other?

JACK:

No, we were both straight. I never saw him again after that cruise.

HENRY:

So you continued on your own.

JACK:

Yeah. It became a habit, I guess. I confessed it a lot; let's just say that.

HENRY:

Well, have you ever heard the old adage, today's trade, tomorrow's competition? I'm sure you have?

JACK:

Yes, I've heard it before.

HENRY:

Well, let's just say there's a lot of truth to it.[sly grin]

JACK:

Why, was that what happened to you?

HENRY:

No. I think I've always been attracted to men from the beginning.

JACK:

I've never been really attracted to men in that way—it was just the blowjobs.

HENRY:

Don't prostitutes give blowjobs?

JACK:

I've never been with one. It just been with men.

HENRY:

Well, there's nothing like sticking with a sure thing.

JACK:

But I'm not sticking with it anymore. I've decided something. I'm going to see the chaplain when I get back. That's why I'm really leaving.

HENRY:

Hmm…what do you think that's going to accomplish?

JACK:

I'll just confess everything, I guess. Get it off my mind. I'm going to truly return to the church. I need a new direction, new moral bearings. I'm going to start new again. That's the only way I can get out of this now.

HENRY:

Well, maybe I should have gotten you a priest this morning instead of Eva.

JACK:

Maybe I wish you had. I've never been out on my wife with another woman. That's what this has brought me to. Now I have no sense of loyalty whatsoever.

HENRY:

Well—that's certainly something someone in your position should seriously think about, I suppose.

JACK:

Why do you care what happens to me now?

HENRY:

I guess because I would want you to stick around longer if you weren't shipping out tomorrow.

JACK:

Well, it's nothing against you. You've been nice. I just have to help myself in the only way I know how. I think it has to come through God.

HENRY:

Everything does. How long is a Med cruise, by the way,

about six months?

JACK:

Yes, more or less.

HENRY:

That's such a beautiful part of the world. It's practically the only place I ever want to go back to, and I'm certain will in a few years.

JACK:

Yes, everybody aboard can't wait to get there, especially the one's who've been before.

HENRY:

But it won't be the same for you. No more looking forward to going ashore.

JACK:

I'll find other things to do. I'll have to.

HENRY:

I wouldn't try and repress it if I were you.

JACK:

All I know is that I have to overpower it.

HENRY:

I don't think it can be *overpowered*—you just *die* and leave it behind.

JACK:

No, I believe that with the help of God and the church anything is possible.

HENRY:

I can't figure out when you decided all this? It must have been while you were shaving.

JACK:

It was. When I looked in the mirror and saw myself.

HENRY:

What was it you saw?

JACK:

Someone who went over the line.

HENRY:

Well, as far as I know there's no going back. And all the Evas in the world aren't going to help you. Nor false excuses.

JACK:

What do you mean false excuses?

HENRY:

Like getting a little high and pretending there's safety in numbers because your buddy did it too. And calling it a habit instead of a desire.

JACK:

That's because I feel bad because I'm married, you know. I would die if my wife found out about any of this.

HENRY:

What if she did? What would she do?

JACK:

It would be the end. She can never know what I've been doing.

HENRY:

What makes you think she doesn't already know?

JACK:

Oh, I'd surely know if she did. She's never suspected anything. Even when we've lived on shore.

HENRY:

Well, what if you had been going out with prostitutes all this time instead of men. Would she forgive you that if she found out?

JACK:

She'd leave me in a minute. You don't know much about married people.

HENRY:

It's hard to avoid them. But let me ask you this: Would she be more willing to forgive you for men or more willing to forgive you for prostitutes?

JACK:

Neither one. Believe me. That's a—stupid question, Henry.

HENRY:

Hmm…maybe not. If you had to make the choice for her, which would you say she could accept more easily?

JACK:

Like I said, neither one. What's this got to do with it?

HENRY:

But, Jack—think for a moment. Your telling your wife you've been unfaithful. Is it going to be with men, or is it going to be with prostitutes? Which one? You must decide—

JACK:

If I had to—[closes his eyes to think] Men, I guess. She'd
resent women more because she is one, I think.

HENRY:

Well, that's a start…

JACK:

What kind of a start?

HENRY:

In case you want to deal with the person involved first rather
than God.

JACK:

You mean really talk to my *wife* about this? There's no way
I could do that, no way. I couldn't disappoint her like that. I
love her. And I want to stay married. I love my kids.

HENRY:

But you also love cock, I think. It wasn't for long, but you
were a natural.

JACK:

That's something I want to forget I ever did.

HENRY:

Now you want to pretend it never happened. Or, even worse,
that it will never happen again.

JACK:

I can never let myself do that again. If I did I could never
kiss my wife!

HENRY:

Well, how have you put your cock in her all these years?

JACK:

That's different in a way…

HENRY:

I can't believe you believe that—

JACK:

Well, I do. Something else I believe too: If I never do it again it will be like it never happened eventually. We do forget things after a while. And once forgotten, they're gone.

HENRY:

That's exactly what the chaplain will tell you, you know. As long as you never do it again you've never done it at all. I don't understand that. Chances are your chaplain is queer himself.

JACK:

I don't know about that. All I know is I don't have any other choice.

HENRY:

There's nothing wrong with you going back to the church if you want, Jack. That's your decision. But I don't think it's going to cure you of your inclinations the way you think it is. Why can't you have your own convictions about this if you think it's wrog?

JACK:

Because God is my conviction.

HENRY:

Well, we're all special to God. Do you think people who starve to death get a special place in Heaven?

JACK:

I don't know. But I hope so.

HENRY:

So do I. I hope you find the answer you're looking for, too.

JACK:

Maybe by the time I get to my next port I'll have found the answer. I've got six more years to go, you know.

HENRY:

Yes, why did you sign up for six more years?

JACK:

For the bonus money, mostly. It's a lot of money. We needed it for a better car and other things.

HENRY:

Yes, but what about the cruises? Aren't they part of the bonus?

JACK:

What do you mean?

HENRY:

It seems to me that the money was for the benefit of your family as a whole, while the cruises are for your benefit alone. Isn't that so? Are you saying that wasn't part of your consideration for signing back up?

JACK:

Well—in the back of my mind maybe. I know it was to some extent. But now—I wish I hadn't signed back up. I wish I wasn't in the navy.

HENRY:

If you wish that it wasn't in the *back* of your mind—I don't think? [sly grin]

JACK:

That wasn't my main reason for signing back up, Henry.

HENRY:

you sure?

JACK:

My family has always come first. Always.

HENRY:

Haven't you simply arranged the lives of your wife and children and yourself so that you could engage in sex with men in ports of call for the next six years? And nobody would be the wiser. Especially yourself.

JACK:

[after a few seconds] Yes. I guess you could say that. [another few seconds] I guess without thinking I've let this rule my life…

HENRY:

Well, *rule* is probably too strong a term. You've simply accommodated it. The best way you knew how.

JACK:

But to go that far—

HENRY:

Some people go further than that—

JACK:

Then I've got no other choice but to go to God.

HENRY:

Hmm…why? To beg him to condemn you? I hope you don't drag me into it!

JACK:

No, to forgive me. And help me change.

HENRY:

Why don't you ask Him to help you understand your situation a little better?

JACK:

I think you've helped me to do that, Henry. Just now.

HENRY:

Well, I've never been on your side of the fence—or a-straddle it as the case may be—but you still have ways of dealing with this.

JACK:

What kind of ways?

HENRY:

I can only tell you how other married people I've known arrange things. So that both sides can live with it. There's lots of cases where the other person knows, but it just discreetly goes without saying, nothing is ever said, and it's just simply put up with for the sake of the marriage. That's—

JACK:

[cutting in] You must be crazy, Henry! I could never let her know anything about this. Even If I *did* continue!

HENRY:

Well, I'm sorry, but I think you will continue. Sooner or later. Don't delude yourself. Like you said, you've gone too far.

JACK:

Now I think you're trying to push me in to this. You know how to create the problem but you don't know how to solve it.

HENRY:

Hmm... I didn't create the problem, Jack.

JACK:

I'm sorry. I know you didn't. I did—no—God did!

HENRY:

I'm not so sure of that. Maybe they should just rewrite the marriage vows—to include things that manifest themselves later on in life.

JACK:

That's just a joke, Henry. I'm sure that's how you meant that.

HENRY:

I think I meant that figuratively.

JACK:

My wife wouldn't care *how* you meant it.

HENRY:

I'm sure you're right. Marriage is so idealized that the good in it can't evolve.

JACK:

I don't want to lose her, Henry. Nor my kids.

HENRY:

Then I suppose you'll have to make the navy a career. It may be after all the honorable thing to do.

JACK:

You're saying one thing and I'm saying another now, Henry. I guess I had better go. I can catch the bus out to the base. [rises, picking up duffel bag]

HENRY:

I hate to see you go, Jack.

JACK:

It's been nice knowing you. [goes toward door]

HENRY:

Well, you too, Jack.

JACK:

Thanks for everything. I hope your cats get okay.

HENRY:

Yes. That reminds me. What was the name of the blind man in the Bible whom the crowd tried to keep away from Jesus? You should know that.

JACK:

[stops, turns] That was Bartimaeus. I'm sure. Why?

HENRY:

Then I shall name the kitten that.

JACK:

That little blind-eyed one?

HENRY:

Yes. I found him on the side of the road. The name Bartimaeus will make him proud of himself. He can be a symbol of the unworthy…the outcast…

JACK:

But Bartimaeus himself didn't think he was – it was the people . . .

HENRY:

Well, neither did the kitten – it was *the people* who set him out. I despise people like that. There's no hope for them.

JACK:

There's always hope, Henry. [goes out]

HENRY:

I hope so.
[HENRY stands there watching the empty door for a moment, then begins taking more stuff out of the box and looking through it. He seems a little sad, but he is intent on what he is doing. This business should take a minute or so, long enough for JACK to get halfway down the street and return, appearing in the doorway looking wild. HENRY looks up surprised.]

JACK:

God, Henry! I had to turn around...

HENRY:

I thought you were going straight.

JACK:

I started shaking again. There's clashes going on in my mind.

HENRY:

Clashes? Well—let's see—I know—why don't you set your bag down and go for a walk. Why don't you do that for now.

JACK:

Why? I was just now walking…

HENRY:

But you weren't looking. You have to look.

JACK:

Look at what?

HENRY:

It doesn't matter what. It's how you look. Look as hard as you can.

JACK:

[setting bag down] Okay. [shrugs] Okay. I'll look. *Hard.*

HENRY:

Take your time.

JACK:

I wonder what time it is?

HENRY:

It's just a little past ten. It's still morning.

JACK:

I seems much later.

HENRY:

I suppose it does. Well, have a nice walk.

JACK:

Maybe I'll walk up to the dock and back.

HENRY:

[quickly] No—ah—why don't you walk toward the beach,

Jack? The breeze will be coming in that way.

JACK:

Okay, I'll walk towards the beach then. [He goes out.]

HENRY:

[Watches him leave, then turns and addresses the audience, thus breaking the spell of the play] A nice walk in the morning sun—there's nothing greater on God's green earth! [sly grin] CURTAIN

NOTES:

www.ingramcontent.com/pod-product-compliance
Lightning Source LLC
Chambersburg PA
CBHW020441290526
45785CB00002B/955